Tourism Employment

Aspects of Tourism

Series Editors: Professor Chris Cooper, *University of Queensland, Ipswich, Australia* and Dr Michael Hall, *University of Otago, Dunedin, New Zealand*

Aspects of Tourism is an innovative, multifaceted series which will comprise authoritative reference handbooks on global tourism regions, research volumes, texts and monographs. It is designed to provide readers with the latest thinking on tourism world-wide and in so doing will push back the frontiers of tourism knowledge. The series will also introduce a new generation of international tourism authors, writing on leading edge topics.

The volumes will be readable and user-friendly, providing accessible sources for further research. The list will be underpinned by an annual authoritative tourism research volume. Books in the series will be commissioned that probe the relationship between tourism and cognate subject areas such as strategy, development, retailing, sport and environmental studies. The publisher and series editors welcome proposals from writers with projects on these topics.

Other Books in the Series
Dynamic Tourism: Journeying with Change
  Priscilla Boniface
Journeys into Otherness: The Representation of Differences and Identity in Tourism
  Keith Hollinshead and Chuck Burlo (eds)
Natural Area Tourism: Ecology, Impacts and Management
  D. Newsome, S.A. Moore and R. Dowling
Tourism Collaboration and Partnerships
  Bill Bramwell and Bernard Lane (eds)
Tourism in Peripheral Areas: Case Studies
  Frances Brown and Derek Hall (eds)
Tourism and Development: Concepts and Issues
  Richard Sharpley and David Telfer (eds)

Please contact us for the latest book information:
Channel View Publications, Frankfurt Lodge, Clevedon Hall,
Victoria Road, Clevedon, BS21 7HH, England
http://www.multilingual-matters.com

ASPECTS OF TOURISM 6
Series Editors: Chris Cooper (*University of Queensland, Australia*)
and Michael Hall (*University of Otago, New Zealand*)

Tourism Employment
Analysis and Planning

Michael Riley, Adele Ladkin
and Edith Szivas

CHANNEL VIEW PUBLICATIONS
Clevedon • Buffalo • Toronto • Sydney

Library of Congress Cataloging in Publication Data
Riley, Michael
Tourism Employment: Analysis and Planning/Michael Riley, Adele Ladkin and
Edith Szivas
Aspects of Tourism: 6
Includes bibliographical references
1. Tourism–Management. 2. Tourism–Personnel management.
3. Tourism–Employees–Supply and demand. I. Ladkin, Adele. II. Szivas, Edith.
III. Title. IV. Series.
G155.A1 L235 2001
910′.68′3–dc21   2001047708

British Library Cataloguing in Publication Data
A catalogue entry for this book is available from the British Library.

ISBN 1-853150-31-8 (hbk)
ISBN 1-853150-30-X (pbk)

Channel View Publications
An imprint of Multilingual Matters Ltd
UK: Frankfurt Lodge, Clevedon Hall, Victoria Road, Clevedon BS21 7SJ.
USA: 2250 Military Road, Tonawanda, NY 14150, USA.
Canada: 5201 Dufferin Street, North York, Ontario, Canada M3H 5T8.
Australia: Footprint Books, Unit 4/92a Mona Vale Road, Mona Vale, NSW 2103, Australia.

Typeset by Florence Production Ltd.
Printed and bound in Great Britain by the Cromwell Press.

Contents

Introduction: The Concept of the Book

There is a twofold purpose to this book. In the first place, it attempts to open up our thinking on tourism employment in order to take it beyond the very important but constrained parameters of managing people in organisations. By the same token it is a plea for more serious study of labour in tourism. If, as is often said, tourism is where the jobs of the future lie, then we need to know a lot more about it. At the same time, the book attempts to widen thinking about manpower planning beyond forecasting estimates to include investigative techniques in a way which may offer insight to economic planning in both tourism and tourism education. These purposes are pursued simultaneously.

The kind of questions that are always asked about tourism include whether it is capable of producing new jobs, why is it relatively low paid and what role should vocational education in this area play? We address these questions but do so indirectly. We seek to contribute to these issues by arguing the importance of understanding tourism labour markets and by showing how they can be understood in a more qualitative way. To this end, we look closely at tourism jobs. We argue that it is helpful to conceive the behaviour of managers and workers as *'industry behaviour'*, or at least *'industry sector behaviour'*, rather than as *'organisational'* or *'occupational'* behaviour in the way management education tends to view it. In support of this perspective we argue that the issues which confront managers and educationalists on a daily basis are contingent upon a wider picture beyond the scope of their specific responsibilities. This argument does not demean the explanatory power of organisational behaviour nor devalue the role of human resource management, but simply suggests that it is the bigger picture that counts! In saying this, it must be clear from the outset that we are not evoking the hegemony of global tourism and corporate strategy. On the contrary, we accept the arguments of Baldacchino (1997) that the local context is

1

a variable in its own right and not just a receptacle for macro-forces such as corporate human resource strategies. We also accept the existence of a small-scale syndrome in many circumstances in the industry. However, in accepting the value of the local context we also accept that the rationale and logic of the wider picture can invade particular circumstance. For example, any macro-level economic rationale can embrace the context of its application without being seriously diverted by it. Similarly, psychological processes are influenced by the context in which they are functioning but operate as independent processes nevertheless. In the sense that we assume that decisions embrace both the specific context and the wider picture we are aligned with 'new institutionalist' concepts (Brinton & Nee, 1998). The wider picture referred to here is essentially the local labour market. Our justification for this stance is that, in this industry, the labour market is dominant and to be truly practical economic forecasts, education policies and the human resource strategies of companies have to be cognisant of its workings. That the labour market is dominant is a major assumption of the book.

From this it might be thought that as the book is about labour markets it must be about macro-level matters – not so! Of the three constructs which form the central plank of our analysis only one, the *labour market* is a macro construct the other two are the *'operating unit'* and *'occupation'*. We superimpose these three constructs upon the tourism industry in order to explore the relationship between its structural dynamics and the behaviour of managers and workers within it. Our analysis seeks the commonality within what is so conspicuously an industry full of diversity.

The sheer size and the scale of its diversity are problematic to the analysis but it is also the rationale for such investigation. Diversity in the industry means that if we are to understand decisions about occupational choice, job mobility patterns or vocational education programmes, a framework has to be found to express both the differences and the commonality within the diverse range of occupations and operating units.

Within this diversity certain structural conflicts exist. One example would be that the interests of the industry and of the operating unit may not be the same and may even be in conflict. In this context we will show how skill is developed through labour mobility – which is a process that sustains the industry and develops the individual but is problematic for the unit. Another example would be the more obvious conflict between the large-scale corporate industry and the small independent sector where the former can often influence the performance of the whole local labour market simply through its size. The need for reconciliation between conflicting interests only emphasises that an understanding of tourism employment requires both a macro and a unit perspective. Invariably tourism industries are fragmented and usually dominated numerically by small units. This aspect of the structure has consequences for labour market dynamics. Furthermore, if tourism employment is to be understood, structure and market interaction needs to be appreciated. Only by seeing the markets in dynamic terms can the major behavioural features of the industry, that is mobility and entrepreneurism, be understood. Static economic and statistical portraits cannot, we argue, capture this.

In the search for commonality within diversity the most obvious candidate is the nature of unit economics. The atomised operating unit, be it a tourist attraction, a hotel, a museum, a travel shop, or whatever, is a central structural variable in our approach. We note that across all tourism sectors, from cruise ships to museums, there is a common dependence upon throughput as the pivotal economic tenet. This leads directly to another source of commonality, for each unit shares, to different degrees, the problem of short-term variations in demand. This is a key feature of the industry which, when taken with the direct nature of demand for labour, means that contingency matching of customer throughput to labour supply is a common mode of labour management. In this context it would be tempting to make a crude generalisation to the effect that labour management is basically a matter of the problems of *expensive cheap labour*. Expensive in the sense that labour is a large cost component; but cheap in that pay levels are relatively low. Whilst largely true, this is a crude generalisation that merits closer examination. Here we base our arguments on the behavioural and psychological implications of easily-learned skills. We use Rosen's (1972) notion of the virtual market wage and Riley's (1991) structural portrait of skill accumulation to examine the inflationary and deflationary pressures on pay against the background of productivity and in a context of fluctuating demand. Our analysis uses both organisational and labour market perspectives.

To an extent, it is the importance we give to the operating unit and to the labour market that allows the analysis to transcend notions of *'developing'* and *'mature'* tourism industries. The two concepts are recognised by our supply side perspective, but in doing so the book also recognises that the incentives inherent in skill differentials can fuel labour migration and act as bridge between old and new tourism industries. Furthermore, in supply-side terms, the global-local construct has a reality in the existence of, on the one hand, international markets for particular skilled employees and on the other, populations of workers who operate solely in a local labour market irrespective of whether or not they migrated to that market.

Our advocacy of investigative techniques is an attempt to convince the reader that it is possible to understand the macro level by looking closely and systematically at the micro level. In this respect the ideas contained in this book are influenced by the writing of George Psacharopoulos (1991a), who argued successfully that the qualitative analysis of labour markets was valuable to forecasting and planning because it could reveal how the present came about. In doing so it could show what patterns remained constant in a changing economic circumstances thus allowing value to be placed on them. It also recognised that the labour market, as a learning resource, is a distinct entity from education, vocational education and formal training. It is this quality in the approach that makes it relevant to the study of tourism employment. This approach to planning is about finding out how a particular level of human capital came about before plans are laid to change it. In focusing on one sector we are evoking the usefulness of sectorial over national analysis, particularly in the areas of skill shortages and training needs (Castley, 1996).

To reiterate, the rationale of the text is that the conventional macro analysis is insufficient to understand tourism employment and that organisational behaviour is an incomplete perspective to understanding working in an industry dominated by labour market forces. An appreciation of the principles of investigative manpower planning, we suggest, is helpful to both. The philosophy and techniques of this approach run as a theme through the text. This is an academic text which is analytical in tone and which looks at behaviour from the perspective of the industry, the unit and the job. It uses economic, sociological and psychological analysis and takes a pragmatic stance on the difficulties of measurement. It offers readers, whether they are students, managers, planners or educationalists an in-depth understanding of tourism employment as a whole and in its specifics.

The book is in three parts. The first section looks at labour in the industry as a whole and concentrates on its primary features, such as diversity, skill, pay and productivity. This section begins in Chapter 1 with a look at the diversity of tourism and the problems for planning and measurement that ensue. Chapter 2 turns around the problem of diversity and sees it in terms of attractiveness and accessibility. Chapters 3 and 4 on productivity and pay are concerned with the economic underpinning of labour management in tourism. Chapter 3 shows the importance of labour to overall productivity and how labour productivity is actually achieved. It goes on to raise the important issue of the relationship between productivity and employment growth. Chapter 4 attempts to explain levels of pay and pay differentials by exploring the deflationary pressures that are exerted on levels of pay by the structure and motives that exist in the tourism industry. It is an attempt to form a conceptual framework for understanding pay determination in the industry. Chapter 5 highlights the nature of service employment and what it implies for the behaviour of managers and workers in the industry. In a sense, Chapter 5 forms the qualitative heart of many of the structural arguments used elsewhere in the book. Motives are entwined in the nature of what people do and the nature of a job determines its labour market characteristics; thus, by this link, a rope bridge is thrown between human agency and structure.

Part 2 begins by establishing the principles of investigative manpower planning. Chapter 6 explores in detail the technique of biographical analysis, which is built upon the notions of autobiographical memory and age distributions. Both concepts are explained. At this point the book presents some examples of the techniques in practice. Chapter 7 describes the theory and practice of qualitative labour market studies and introduces the principal behavioural construct of our analysis: mobility. Chapters 6–12 are essentially a series of studies over a range of tourism employment areas, which include motivation, mobility and classification of job content.

Part 3 attempts to examine the implications of sections one and two for policy making in three important areas. Chapter 13 examines the implications for human resource management and organisational structure and Chapter 14 reflects upon tourism education in the light of what has gone before. In other words, after outlining the big picture, explored the rational for, and techniques of, investigative manpower planning and having giving some empirical examples we return to the pragmatic issues of managing people and educating people. The book concludes (Chapter 15) by revisiting planning and development in the light of the approaches outlined in the text.

Part 1

Understanding the Industry

Chapter 1
Diversity and Planning: The Dynamic Nature of the Industry

Introduction

The intention in Chapter 1 is to introduce problems that the tourism industry bequeaths to those intending to undertake any form of planning or research in relation to labour and education. The point is not to deter but to forewarn and to encourage realism in the outputs of studies.

Difficulties in Defining Tourism

Like any other form of research or planning, labour planners come across the first hurdle – what is tourism? After decades of research in the field, it is surprising how difficult it is to reach a universally meaningful definition of tourism. Numerous attempts have been made so far – both from the supply and the demand side but finding a universally applicable definition for tourism is hampered by a number of other factors. Some of the difficulties in finding a definition are outlined in Table 1.1.

Tourism is not a recognised industry in the Standard Industrial Classification (Cooper *et al.*, 1998) and most countries' national accounts would not list tourism as a separate entity. In most statistical systems the best approximation we can get on tourism (and especially on tourism employment) is to look up the restaurant and catering entry. This, of course, is largely due to the fact that tourism is seen as an industry dominated by the hospitality sector.

However, tourism does not only consist of the hospitality sector and any planner must be aware of the fact that tourism is a *'multiproduct industry'* with strong linkages to other economic sectors (Diamond, 1977). Probably the most obvious example for this inter-linkage is the transport industry where most businesses share their operation between the

Table 1.1 Difficulties in defining tourism

- Tourism is often not recognised as an industry
- Strong linkages with other economic sectors
- Diverse, with a range of inter-linked sectors
- Tourist use – local use mix
- Informal economy
- Traditionally seen as dominated by hotel sector
- Paucity of statistics
- Differing interpretations between countries as to what constitutes a tourist trip

Table 1.1 gives an outline of why tourism is such a hard industry to pin down. Often the official status of 'a recognised industry' is not conferred on tourism even when it is a major contributor to national GDP. To some extent this is explainable by the fact that it has many connections to other economic sectors and that, within itself, it has many sectors with permeable borders. To complicate matters further, the use of tourist facilities is rarely exclusive to tourists which makes the measurement of such concepts as impact that much harder.

two sectors. To illustrate the point, consider to what extent, for example, taxi or coach companies are part of tourism?

The paucity of tourism statistics or at least their incompleteness is strongly inter-linked with the above discussed points. The dominance of the hospitality sector and the difficulty in drawing the boundaries of tourism encourage the view that the magnitude of tourism can be estimated from data on the hospitality sector. But the opposite is also true; in the absence of comprehensive data, we often resort to using hospitality-related data and narrow the discussion to the hotel and catering industries. Given the diversity in the tourism industry, this practice inevitably restricts our view of the industry and can lead to conclusions that are only partially true.

The true dimensions of the tourism industry clearly stretch beyond the hospitality sector as the industry would not function without a number of other sectors and operators who together form this complex industry. Any plan should take into account that apart from hotels, the tourism industry also includes a number of other sectors and activities, namely:

- Transport.
- Tour operators, travel agencies.
- Tourist attractions.
- Conference business.
- Tour guides.

- Tourist information services.
- Souvenir shops, beach vendors.
- Relevant government offices.
- NGOs.
- Educational establishments.

In addition to the above points, there is also the added complexity that arises from the fact that most tourist facilities are, in fact, shared between the tourists and the locals. The extent to which facilities are shared between 'hosts' and 'guests' is largely influenced by the economic distance between them and the type of tourism at the destination. Whatever the proportion of tourist usage, the important question is how do we decide which hotel or tourist attraction or shop is part of the tourism industry and which one is not?

It will come as no surprise that, as tourism is difficult to pin down, then defining tourism employment has its own problems. Just who is employed in tourism?

Defining Tourism Employment

When attempting to define tourism employment a useful starting point is supply-side definitions as they approach tourism as an aggregate of businesses and organisations. For example, a supply-side definition by Leiper (1979) states that:

> the tourist industry consists of all those firms, organisations and facilities which are intended to serve the specific needs and wants of the tourists. (p. 400).

The definition is clear but it is only when we try to collate a list of these facilities for a manpower survey or labour market analysis that we realise the inherent difficulties in finding the boundaries of tourism employment (Szivas, 1999). Some of the issues are summarised below:

- Apart from the obvious choices such as hotels and travel agents, we find that most companies and establishments serve not only tourists but also locals. Restaurants, tourist attractions, taxis and other forms of transport all fall into this latter category. Recognising this, Smith (1988) classified facilities and firms serving the tourists into two levels: one tier encompasses all those establishments whose total revenue is derived from tourists, while on a second tier are those businesses which serve both the tourists and the locals as well. For our manpower survey we might opt to include those operators whose business is totally dependent on serving the tourists but by opting for this, we exclude the majority of businesses. This is especially true for developing countries where the patronage of tourism facilities is predominantly from the international tourist.

- The complexity and the neglect with which tourism is often handled at official levels means that there is no precise definition. This leads to a lack of statistics to quantify the dimensions of tourism employment (World Tourism Organisation, 1983). Consequently, the exact boundaries of tourism employment are as difficult to draw as it is to define tourism itself (Burns, 1993).
- The discussion on tourism employment tends to be focused on hotel employment. This clearly simplifies matters but has serious shortcomings as the boundaries of the industry stretch beyond the hotel sector and tourist expenditure also occurs in restaurants, shops and recreational facilities. Furthermore, tourists also use transportation and financial services, contributing to the relevant economic sectors both in their home country and at the tourist destination. They also engage in activities such as hunting or bird watching which affect the agriculture sector whilst purchases are also made in retail outlets, impacting upon the retail sector.
- In most tourist companies, part of the workforce is directly involved with dealing with the tourists, while others have no direct contact with them. If we try to define tourism employment as an aggregate of people who have direct contact with tourists we are excluding professionals such as accountants, maintenance people and baggage handlers!
- Finally, another problem in defining the boundaries of tourism employment is the prevalence of the informal economy in tourism (Shaw & Williams, 1994). Multiple occupations further complicate the matter leading to misleading employment data (Cukier-Snow & Wall, 1993).

Given the above considerations, if tourism establishments are going to be used as indicators of tourism employment then a careful set of assumptions needs to be set up for interpreting the results. The kind of variables that need to be defined are: sector of tourism, type of establishment, location and inclusive occupational titles. Clearly, to define these variables requires any study of tourism to have a 'working definition' at the outset. This stricture becomes even more significant when account is taken of the extent of diversity within the industry.

Diversity in the Tourism Industry

Given the breath of the industry implied above, the greatest source of diversity must come from the diverse jobs associated with different sectors of the industry. At the establishment level there is diversity in size, business type and in the extent of fluctuation of customer demand. Even within sectors there is considerable organisational diversity. This is accompanied at the occupational level by a huge variety of occupations and skills (International Labour Office, 1989b). It is therefore not surprising that forms of employment, contractual obligations, working conditions and pay vary considerably between sectors and within sectors and by organisational size across all sectors (Burns, 1993).

This diversity, be it sectoral, functional, organisational, or process is linked to a diversity of job types which in turn ensure a variety of different types of workers employed in the industry. Even given the same job its content may vary by the context in which it exists. Standard of service, size of enterprise, type of product, type of clientele, location, seasonality and required level of skills are all differentiating factors. Although tourism is seen as a service industry it would be wrong to assume that all workers are actually undertaking service tasks. In the parlance of operational research, the variety of tasks includes materials processing, customer processing and information processing. Additionally, there are variations in employment status. The industry offers jobs both on a full-time and part-time basis and requires stable and casual, seasonal and migrant labour (International Labour Office, 1989a).

Even within occupational diversity there is process diversity. At the simplest level there are manufacturing tasks, service tasks and information processing tasks and these are sometimes duplicated within one job. Across this typology we have to lay the dimensions of mass, batch and individual. Adding to this diversity is the modern operational management approach of mass customisation where mass demand is satisfied only by quasi-individualised products and services.

The implications of such diversity on planning and research are that information about jobs must be surrounded by descriptive variables that place the job in its correct industrial context. We cannot make judgements of any kind upon labour data unless it is sufficiently comprehensive. To illustrate why this is necessary take the occupation receptionist in the context of a pay survey. Job title and rate of pay convey nothing unless we also know the sector, organisational size, class of establishment and associated skill requirements. Often a considerable number of variables are needed to capture diversity. These variables include: job title, job content, job tenure, level of pay, level of skill, sector employed, type of organisation, size of organisation, status or class of organisation. These are the standard tenets of any occupational classification scheme and further discussion of the mechanics and problems of such classifications are found in Chapter 10. Manpower planning always needs a classification scheme and the general rule is that it must be capable of capturing the level of anticipated diversity. The good news is that they become easier where common skills cross sectors, which is the case in tourism. The bad news is that all classification schemes capture a static picture. The problem that remains is to cope with the dynamics, the moving parts of an industry.

The Industry Environment

In a sense the most important dynamic force in tourism is its labour market expressed by patterns of mobility. Furthermore, an element that is equally relevant to planning is the existence of a complex set of dichotomies that characterise the industry. Some built-in dichotomies are illustrated in Table 1.2.

'Tourism exemplifies many aspects of globalisation' (Brown, 1998: 18) yet at most destinations multinational firms operating on the global scale co-exist with large numbers of local businesses. In addition to this, the industry is characterised by a dual structure where large operators co-exist with a multitude of small, often family owned businesses.

Although technological change is inevitable in the industry, in many operations high-tech and low-tech live together – E-bookings for the hotel chains, telephone bookings for the bed and breakfast operations;

Table 1.2 The industry environment

- Global – local dimensions
- Dual structure: important chains and numerous independents
- Range of sizes and standards
- Geographically fragmented structure
- High tech and low tech live together
- Entrepreneurial ethos – way of life motivation

These dichotomies represent real contrasts that make a difference to working lives in the industry. Perhaps the overarcing dichotomy is that between the entrepreneurial ethos and the need for planning. Both are essential but are not easy bedfellows.

or management for the front-of-house but a low level of technological sophistication for housekeeping. Some people go into tourism to be successful entrepreneurs others see it as a *'way of life'*. These dichotomies do not hinder labour planning but simply make it more complex. For example, predicting rates of growth, levels of productivity and the take up of new technology will be influenced by the proportions of corporate to independent entrepreneurs in the field. There is always a certain tension between the formalities and the planning process in relation to tourism projects and the entrepreneurial spirit that lies behind them.

Perhaps more important for tourism employment planning is the dynamic nature of the labour market. In almost all sectors it is characterised by: occupational diversity; high proportions of young people – many in their first job; relatively low pay; an unreliable relationship between pay and tenure and between pay and skill; high levels of mobility of all types, but particularly inter-organisational mobility and upward mobility. In other words, the labour market is dynamic and, along with employers and education, a major independent player in the provision of employment. The characteristics of the market will be developed further in Chapters 4 and 5. The characteristics of the dynamic nature of the market that make difficulties for planning are outlined in Table 1.3.

Table 1.3 Difficulties for planners

- Highly elastic wage-employment relationship
- Wide range of earnings in skilled occupations
- An ability to 'cope'by improvisation which distorts productivity measures
- High labour mobility between units
- Low occupational mobility
- Seasonality

What these features mean is that some of the key pieces of data and objectives in manpower planning are hard to obtain, for example:

- Estimating the returns to education, which are the basis of cost-benefit calculations in educational investment, is obscured first, by the partial detachment of pay from level of skill and second by the lack of credentialism in the industry.
- Levels of productivity are hard to estimate first because of the stochastic nature of demand and second by the differential and partial impact of new technology.

- The task of making comparisons in the industry is made difficult by the diversity within any single job title.

Conclusion

In this chapter we discussed some basic issues that planners and researchers need to be aware of when exploring labour market issues in tourism. Further aspects of the notion of diversity and dynamics will be addressed in the following chapters. The intention in the following chapters will be to clarify the detail of some of the issues involved and to suggest ways in which investigative techniques of manpower planning can offer solutions.

Chapter 2
Attraction and Accessibility

Introduction

It could be suggested that, in a sense, tourism employment is blighted by the confusing complexity of its own image. On the one hand, the image of tourism employment is of glamour while, on the other hand, there is evidence of low pay and low status. As with all images, there is both truth and fiction in its components. Yet images count in terms of both the quantity and quality of an industry's labour force. To understand the effect of images of employment, it is necessary to understand the flow of labour into and out of tourism. This process has two related components – the attractiveness or unattractiveness of the industry to potential employees and the accessibility of jobs and careers. Attractiveness alone will not explain the patterns which we see. How easy or difficult it is to enter tourism employment matters as well!

Attractiveness and Accessibility: Are They Related Concepts?

Any initial analysis of the attractiveness of an industry as an employer is almost certain to focus on the character of the work and the occupations. Common sense would suggest that there are bound to be certain negative characteristics of tourism employment, which have to be considered and balanced against the attractive characteristics. There is an issue here that research has rather neglected which is, whether it is a person's concept of the industry or their image of a particular job that forms the focus of the attraction. In terms of accessibility, it will be the structure of the industry that determines the opportunity structure. This is true for all industries but here again there is an issue. How do people on the outside see the opportunity structure of an industry as diverse as

17

tourism? In the absence of hard evidence on both these issues the safe assumption would be that interested individuals would focus on the nature of the work and the level of its technology as a measure of skill requirements.

We argue that the dimensions of attractiveness and accessibility work together. Attractiveness carries with it an implication of accessibility, without which occupational choice becomes just dreaming. At the very least, any individual superficially attracted to an occupation will make an assessment of his or her personal chances of obtaining the job and being successful in it. In similar vein, accessibility carries connotations of attractiveness. It might be very easy to access a job nobody else wants, because it is seen as an awful job! The reverse is also likely to be true.

At one level it would be easy to assume that attractiveness is only a matter of the intrinsic characteristics of a job. This is not true. Just as the notion of job satisfaction is made up of intrinsic and extrinsic attributes combined in a process, so is occupational image. The attributes of a job, which form its image to those who might show interest in it, include extrinsic attributes such as pay and status. Markets, as we know work, on information and that information often comes in the form of reputation and image. For those with experience, the information contained in an image can be interpreted, but for potential newcomers this is not the case. The industry takes in a large proportion of first-jobbers, therefore image plays a key role in recruitment and standards.

The Image of Occupations and Market Relations

The image of occupations is an important stimulus in career choice decisions. One way to look at the image of an occupation is a fusion of certain components:

- the duties which have to be carried out by its practitioners;
- the occupation's contribution to society;
- the level of remuneration it is reputed to receive;
- the lifestyle enjoyed by those in the occupation.

In other words, the reputation of an occupation is related to both its content and its wider setting, particularly its social prestige (Coxon & Jones, 1978). Occupational titles are social currency and, therefore, given this relationship of occupations to social prestige, it is not surprising that occupations with poor image tend to be unattractive, whereas occupations which enjoy positive image are attractive. However, the relationships within this fusion may not be congruent and can be the subject of 'trade-offs'. In other words, the job satisfaction process of trading-off attributes applies to images as well. Although status and earnings are clearly linked together, they can move in separate directions. It is possible to trade a decrease in status for higher pay or accept lower pay in order to possess higher status. People might give up higher prestige occupations for lower prestige jobs if they are compensated by higher pay, higher job satisfaction or by convenience factors.

Again, it would be easy to assume that the image of an occupation is always clear and unambiguous even when that image has the status of a generally accepted reputation. This is not so, nor is an image necessarily permanent. If occupations are linked to social prestige then it follows that occupational prestige hierarchies may vary with social cultures. It most certainly varies amongst individuals. The fact that different individuals can have different images of the same occupation can not only be attributed to different propensities but also to a different stock of experiences and observations (Ossowski, 1963 cited in Coxon & Jones, 1978).

The way people perceive the external reality is through themselves and the social structure which he or she is part of. In this sense the 'self' acts as a boundary to the recognition of the outside world (Neisser, 1967) This brings to the fore the role of experience in image construction and reception. When people from different industries and with different career histories and educational backgrounds take up jobs in tourism, they are likely to have different images of the same tourism occupations. This might account for differential levels of interest in particular tourism jobs.

Notwithstanding such differences, these images form expectations that in their turn affect the way the individual feels about the job and performs the job. Experience brings reality into occupational decisions but, to be fair to the concept of the image, even glamorous images contain a reputational *'reality'* which conditions the gloss.

The role of attractiveness in recruitment lies in its ability to influence the supply side. In this respect the image may attract suitable people but it also has the power to deter suitable people and attract the unsuitable. Image is a market player! Accessibility has a similar inducing and deterring role but it has other properties as well. The ease or difficulty of access also affects the *value placed on the occupation*. Easy access to an occupation, for example, could mean that potential incumbents place a low value on that occupation. This line of argument would be supported by Human Capital Theory in which people seek rewards from occupations that are appropriate to the personal investment that has been made is securing knowledge and skill (see Chapter 7).

Finally, and perhaps the most dangerous implication of occupational images is that they are a substitute for factual knowledge. Given that perfect information is never available in the market, incorrect reputational knowledge can have an adverse affect on occupational choice and in the process of matching supply to demand. In these circumstances it is worth asking just how important an occupational image actually is. If an image becomes, for whatever reason, detached from the reality it may be damaging in a number of ways. The impact of such damage would be on those people contemplating tourism employment or new entrants to the industry. The image could hide opportunities or attractive characteristics and conversely, it could also hide an unattractive reality. By doing so, it could deter suitable people and break the expectations of newcomers causing disillusionment. It is one of the soundest tenets of the selection process that realistic expectations are the basis of long-term employment relationships. If it is so important, can a poor image be reconstructed? At this point the structure of the industry re-enters the equation. Essentially, the more fragmented the industry, the harder it becomes to marshal the cooperative effort to change an image. Image management is facilitated by centralisation.

The Image of Tourism Employment

The image of tourism employment appears to be split: on the one hand tourism jobs possess a certain image of glamour, while on the other hand, they are deemed as of low status and of low skill. In the UK context, a report by the National Economic Development Council (1992) on the UK tourism labour market states that the positive characteristics attributed to tourism by career teachers include opportunities to travel, meeting people, foreign language use and variety. However, the report also suggests that the industry's traditional image of low pay, long hours and minimal training still prevail. Meeting people and travel are often seen as glamorous and attractive aspects of tourism employment and in a sense they compete in the image stakes with negative aspects such as low pay, service and menial status.

In the general tourism literature the industry is described as a low-skill employer (Mathieson & Wall, 1982; Jafari *et al.*, 1990). A report by the International Labour Office (1989: 9) states that despite the improvement in the overall image of the industry in recent years, 'in some countries the sector is not yet viewed favourably as an employer owing to poor employment and working conditions and high levels of unskilled employment'. Jobs in tourism are often seen as 'menial and low level for unskilled hands' (Brachmann, 1988 cited in Sindiga, 1994), and many of them are regarded as demeaning.

Tourism jobs often require lower levels of qualification, pay low wages and therefore it is not surprising if tourism employment in general does not enjoy high status. The tourism employee is often seen as 'uneducated, unmotivated, untrained, unskilled and unproductive' (Pizam, 1982: 5).

Given the complexity of tourism itself which results in a wide range of occupations, it is plausible to suggest that there is considerable variation in the image of particular tourism occupations and that the image of the industry as an employer might differ from that of certain tourism jobs. *We may add to this argument that, given the evidence of market determination of pay, the reputed low levels of pay are not the complete story and that the industry contains many well paid occupations* (see Chapter 4). In a way, the diversity and sectoral fragmentation of tourism, which makes life so difficult for the task of image improvement, does act to ensure that the poor image of some occupations does not automatically transfer to all tourism occupations.

Hotel work, for example, is often associated with marginality which causes serious and unfair damage to the image of the related occupations. Hotel work is often viewed as an occupation for drifters (Saunders, 1981) and socially or psychologically marginal people (Mars *et al.*, 1979). The veracity of the marginality argument has to contend with the sheer numbers of people employed in the hotel industry. It is doubtful if such numbers could count as marginal! Alpert (1986) also draws a rather unfavourable picture, this time of the US restaurant labour force. People working in this category tend to be young, without family obligations and less well educated than the typical worker. For most employees, the sector is not a career option, but rather a preparation for a career in another section of the economy. Alpert sees the type of work as predominantly a women's sector for whom it provides a convenient opportunity to gain work experience, training and some income.

A quite different argument is made by Corcoran and Johnson (1974) who suggest that it is the service element of hotel work that is responsible for the low image. They found that career teachers saw the job of cooks and chefs as having a favourable image while the jobs of room maids, waiters and porters were had an unfavourable image. An international research project – 'Tourism as a Factor of Change: A Sociocultural Study' fostered by the Vienna Centre, which encompassed seven countries (Bulgaria, Hungary, Poland, Spain, United Kingdom, United States and Yugoslavia) found that generally, tourism jobs did not possess a great deal of status and respect and the most respected occupations in the industry were hotel and restaurant managers, tourist guides and mountain refuge managers. A significant finding in the study is that despite the image problem, the majority of the respondents in each country expressed a willingness to take up a job in tourism (Jafari *et al.*, 1990).

A useful analysis of the status of jobs and professions across the different sectors of tourism and across a number of countries is provided in a report by the World Tourism Organisation (1983). In broad terms, the findings on the major tourism occupations were as follows:

> The study found that government organisation professions generally enjoy good status which probably results from the entry requirements, career opportunities and conditions of employment. In the accommodation sector, managers and supervisors enjoy an improved status which is the result of growth in organisational size, higher entry requirements, development of vocational education and training and the involvement of regulatory and voluntary bodies. Lower level jobs in the sector do not enjoy similar positive characteristics. Many occupations in the transport sector and particularly those in the air transport segments enjoy favourable status. Those whose work is related to tourist attractions and entertainment facilities rarely enjoy high status, the exception being those associated with the most prestigious tourist attractions. In the tour operator segment those engaged in central operations enjoy reasonable status because of the career opportunities they have, whereas the field staff suffer from low status. The status of travel agency occupations is generally relatively low. The status of tourist guides varies from country to country. They tend to be self-employed, often work only part-time or seasonally. In some countries it provides career opportunity, in others it is seen as an opportunity to travel before settling down. The status of guides is enhanced by the fact that the work usually requires considerable language skills. The status of the job is the highest in countries with strong cultural values and where the entry requirements into the profession are high.

The variation in the appraisal and image of tourism occupations is probably most apparent in the comparison of developing and developed economies. Cukier-Snow and Wall (1993) note that although most hotel jobs are menial, in developing countries they pay better wages than occupations in agriculture and are, therefore, appraised relatively favourably. It is well documented that in these countries the younger generation prefer tourism jobs rather than work in traditional industries. Diamond (1977) points out that the appraisal of the skill level of tourism jobs is not an absolute and depends on the general skill and educational level of the country.

A general conclusion on the image of tourism occupations might be that behind the obvious contrast of glamour on the one hand and low menial status on the other, lies a great deal of ambiguity. Furthermore, it is clear that images show variation between countries and depend on the circumstances of the person who makes the judgement. However, the evidence suggests that the image of tourism employment is generally closely identified with the actual work undertaken rather than evolving from some culturally-influenced national occupational prestige hierarchy. The implication of this is that actual experience of tourism work is influential on the construction of the image in general and on personal interpretations.

The Characteristics of Tourism Employment which Determine its Attractiveness

Putting aside all considerations of image, tourism employment does possess certain qualities which make it attractive for those considering tourism employment. The accessibility of tourism occupations is one such factor. The industry accommodates those with a great variety of skills, with low skill levels or with non-relevant skills. In other words, tourism employment might be attractive because of the relative ease of entry.

The constant fluctuations of consumer demand in tourism, both in terms of quantity and quality, result in a work environment where routine plays a minor role and where improvisation and flexibility are important parts of the job. When compared to monotonous occupations such as factory work where the factory line dictates and where the work is impersonal and mechanic, tourism occupations might offer a more attractive alternative for many. This is supported by Riley (1986b) who found a strong element of *'not factory'* in the orientation of hotel workers to their industry. The lack of routine and close supervision awoke a positive attitude amongst employees to their low-paid work.

A distinct characteristic of tourism work is that the boundaries between work and leisure time are often obscured. Marshall (1986 cited in Urry, 1990 and Shaw & Williams, 1994) found that restaurant employees did not see their job as real work because of the strong amalgamation of work and leisure. In hotel and restaurant work part of the working hours constitute leisure when customers, many of whom are friends or acquaintances, are entertained. Furthermore, much of leisure time is spent at the work-place, further obscuring the boundaries between work and leisure. This suggests that businesses like restaurants might gain loyalty of their peripheral employees from the fact that the *'symbolic boundaries between work and leisure'* are weak.

The fact that a large proportion of tourism jobs involve direct contact with customers is to some, an attractive aspect of tourism work. While it has to be acknowledged that the high level of interpersonal contact involved in tourism jobs does have negative consequences (Mathieson & Wall, 1982; Shamir, 1981), it is attractive for those who enjoy dealing with people. Mars *et al.* (1979, cited in Wood, 1992: 18) suggest that the hotel industry tends to attract those who '. . . derive satisfaction in situations in which a large number of ephemeral but jovial relationships can be made'.

As labour flexibility is at the very heart of tourism employment it is worth debating whether or not this can be counted as an attractive aspect of the industry. Given the seasonal and periodic variations in demand in tourism, seasonal (Ball, 1989) and part-time work is common in the industry (Jafari *et al.*, 1990; International Labour Office, 1989). This inevitably has a negative effect on job security, career prospects and pay and makes tourism employment unattractive for those who are looking for permanent full-time jobs with clear career opportunities. However, there is another side of the coin in that it can be argued that part-time and seasonal work might be attractive for certain segments of the labour market simply because it is flexible. Women and students are cited most often to take up part-time work opportunities, while seasonal jobs are also thought to attract people from the periphery of the labour force (Mathieson & Wall, 1982). Shaw and Williams (1994) point out that despite the inevitable inconvenience caused by unpredictable variations in work and the insecure nature of part-time and seasonal employment, there is a certain attraction attached to such occupations. They suggest that two factors be considered. First, that often there is no better alternative job in the local labour market and second, that non-material benefits like accommodation, tips and the psychological income derived from working and sometimes living in an attractive environment provides a valuable trade-off for low wages and insecure jobs. Furthermore, the social expectation of women to have dual careers as mothers and family caretakers means that they are unavailable for full-time jobs or can only be engaged in occupations with flexible working hours.

While tourism employment might be attractive for a number of reasons, the issue of reputed low pay has to be addressed. Chapter 4 discusses the causes of low pay in the industry. However, caution has to be made when condemning the industry for low pay. The lack of information hides the many instances of high pay in the industry and in some occupations basic pay is often supplemented by fringe benefits, such as: subsidised food and lodging, tips and 'fiddles', a fact which cannot be ignored (Alpert, 1986; Wood, 1992). One of the strangest aspects of tourism occupations is the regular reporting of high job satisfaction coexisting with low pay – an issue addressed in Chapter 4.

Attributes of the Industry and its Accessibility

How accessible is the tourism industry for those wishing to join it either as a first job or from other industries? We suggest that it is very accessible because of the accommodating nature of tourism.

The multifaceted diversity described in Chapter 1, infects functions, organisations and skills. Tourism offers a wide variety of jobs with diverse human capital requirements. We argue that such variety might be attractive when viewed with inter-industry mobility in mind. People with varying pre-tourism work experience might find something suitable for themselves. The fact that the industry can accommodate a wide range of skills can be seen as an enticing characteristic for those who want to or have to move away from non-tourism employment (Szivas & Riley, 1999).

In this connection it is often argued, particularly in the hotel and restaurant sector, that the skills needed are those which women obtain naturally outside of their jobs in their role as wives and mothers, therefore women can join the industry for certain occupations without any formal training. Tasks like serving meals, working in kitchens and making beds are similar to those undertaken in the household and similar jobs in hotels are traditionally regarded as female occupations (Shaw & Williams, 1994). This view is largely capitalised on in developing countries with low levels of education and large numbers of women outside the formal labour market.

Although skill is a relative concept, the nature of the skills in tourism is such that they can be easily learnt *'on the job'* and consequently employers often take on unskilled labour and rely on *'on the job training'*. This means that not only is entry comparatively easy but there is also a promise of skill development within the industry. This implied promise of development is part of the ethos of the industry. Becoming a manager or an owner is part of the general incentive of the work.

The notion of acquiring skills for entrepreneurship is part of the industry's attractiveness because it offers opportunity with low capital.

Growth comes through small businesses and furthermore, the structure of tourism is encouraging in a number of ways. First, it is labour intensive. Second, it is responsive to changes in demand and fashion that may be more visible to those working in the industry than those outside it. Third, the largely cash and personal credit basis of transactions allows for market testing without enormous investment. Finally, the presence of large numbers of small-scale enterprises makes it difficult to enforce statuary requirements that constrain large scale organisations. Small tourism businesses often operate in the shadow of the informal economy. Consequently, tourism entrepreneurship, tourism employment and the informal economy are often linked together. Cukier and Wall (1994) state that a substantial portion of tourism employment in developing countries occurs in the informal sector. The informal sector is characterised by 'ease of entry, dependence on indigenous resources, family ownership, small scale of operation, non-formal training of workers, unregulated and competitive markets and intensive labour' (Kermath & Thomas, 1992 cited in Cukier & Wall, 1994). In other words, entry into the tourism industry and into entrepreneurship might be facilitated by the informal economy. These conditions enable those working in the industry to test the market, acquire rudimentary skills and accumulate a small amount of capital which, can later be used for the purposes of establishing a small private business. For example chefs are noted for becoming owners of restaurant businesses. In the case of small accommodation establishments, the business function is combined with the provision of a family home (Shaw & Williams, 1994).

What makes the industry accessible is the skill and job diversity. The process is further facilitated by the diversity of organisations and occupations which encourages mobility. Constant organisational and occupational mobility creates regular vacancies for newcomers.

Conclusion

The arguments of attractiveness and accessibility have to be set against the competitive conditions that prevail. If we return to the original argument over whether it is the industry or the occupation that attracts, this raises the question of the role played by perceptions of the attraction of an industry in growth. It is plausible to suggest that industries that are expanding will get a good reputation in the marketplace and take labour from other industries especially, declining ones. Low entry barriers in the expanding industry clearly facilitate mobility. Tourism satisfies both requirements for mobility; it is growing and it has relatively low human capital requirements. However, if growth is to be an attraction it is necessary for individuals to perceive it. Tourism has an advantage in this respect in that it is conspicuous. People can see coach loads of tourists and new hotels under construction. In other words, growth, image, accessibility and attractiveness of the tourism industry work closely together. The decision, whether to enter the industry for employment, is influenced by factors which interact and feed back to each other.

Chapter 3
Labour Productivity

Introduction

It may, at first glance, seem rather restrictive to look solely at labour productivity when labour is only one element of productivity. However, the rationale for this partial view of productivity comes from the adopted perspective that is, on the one hand, a micro-level focus and on the other, an emphasis on 'achieving productivity' in an operational sense. This contrasts with the more usual perspective of a macro-level economic one with an emphasis on measurement. It will be argued that this micro focus gives a clearer understanding of the significance of labour as a factor in productivity. In other words, it will be suggested that, in the context of tourism labour, macro-level comparative studies using standard regression methods, tend to hide rather than illuminate the contribution of, and problems associated with, labour and total productivity. The other argument in support of the micro perspective is that although industry productivity matters, such productivity is actually 'made' by a fragmented structure of units of varying size. It is at the unit level that productivity connects directly to managerial strategies.

The Problems and Limitations of Macro-Level Comparative Studies

Studies of comparative productivity at the macro-level tend to suffer from problems of equivalence and interpretation. What this means is that, on the one hand, it is hard to make like-for-like comparisons and on the other, explanations of differences often require qualitative data which are outside the remit of the regression analysis.

Attempts have been made to overcome the equivalence problem by using organisational classification systems, marketing classifications and price classifications. These approaches are helpful but incomplete. Studies in the hotel sector, for example, often find conspicuous differences even when size and brand identity has been established (Prais *et al.*, 1989). Factors such as age of the property, proportion of rooms to food and beverage activity and many other idiosyncratic factors make interpretation that much more difficult. The truth is probably that, in macro-scale studies, it is doubtful whether exact equivalence would ever be possible. 'Adequately similar' is probably the most that can be expected.

In the case of qualitative explanations, it is necessary for the study design to anticipate these, otherwise they become just speculative. This is, however, difficult to incorporate into large-scale methodologies. Qualitative variables such as human capital inputs have to be reduced to quantifiable 'levels' which often fail to represent the variety present in the situation. It is not uncommon to find credentials used to represent human capital as a whole. In the case of tourism this would certainly be inadequate.

Notwithstanding the problems of equivalence and qualitative variables, the more serious consideration is that of how to measure output. In common with other industries, the output of tourism units can be expressed by generic measures such as value added, by physical measures such as throughput or occupancy or, by financial measures such as revenue and profitability (Baker *et al.*, 1992). From a macro perspective these measures look fine but at the micro-level their shortcomings and inadequacy become apparent. In essence, the argument is that in tourism it is variations in demand in the very short-term that govern productivity rather than the level of demand represented by any of the conventional output measures. Macro-level models do not capture the effects of short-term changes in demand and it is for this reason that they fail to describe the contribution of labour. To understand this, it is necessary to look at the fundamental concept of productivity as it applies to tourism units.

The Concept of Productivity

The standard assumption of a productivity analysis is expressed in terms of an input-output model where the level of inputs determines the output. Tourism activities, however, exhibit the reverse of this assumption. In other words, in tourism, output drives input. A similar position is found in health care units where rate of illness and case mix drives the utilisation of medical resources. The standard and reverse concepts of productivity are not inconsistent; they simply exist at different levels and with different spans of explanation (Riley, 1999). The initial feasibility of most tourism and hospitality operations is built around estimated throughput but *when up and running the importance of throughput does not diminish.* It is often said that the customer is king but, in the sphere of productivity, the *throughput* of customers is always king.

From the above, it follows that variations in demand are the key factor in operational productivity. If demand varies in the short term, then supply inputs need to match that variation in the cause of productivity.

An Anatomy of the Problem

The implications of accepting the idea that demand governs supply is that the achievement of any level of operational productivity is a matter of forecasting accurately and responding effectively to that demand. From the perspective of the unit, this problem can be seen as three types of uncertainty, namely:

*   How many customers will arrive?
*   What will be consumed from what has been offered and prepared?
*   When will consumption take place?

The response of management to such uncertainty is, on the one hand, to reduce it through standardisation policies and accurate forecasting and on the other hand, to make resources as flexible as possible. These approaches would together form a platform of a managerial strategy on productivity. However the problem is more complicated. In labour-intensive industries the actual abilities and motivations of individual workers makes a difference to productivity and furthermore as labour is not totally flexible there is always the need for a residual level of employment in each unit irrespective of changes in demand. In the light of this, the problem can be restated as the need to:

*   Increase individual productivity.
*   Match labour supply to variable demand.
*   Minimise the residual level of employment.

These imperatives are not separate issues, they are part of the same thing. Perhaps the best way to understand the interrelationship between these three aspects of productivity is to look at the processes that influence the relationship between them. This relationship involves four related concepts – human capital, technological substitution, labour substitution and product/service diversity-standardisation. The relationship between the last three is given coherence by their common link to human capital. By human capital is meant the sum of an individual's education training and experience, and as a variable it displays certain 'levels'. Getting the 'appropriate level' is a matter related to hiring and training policies. For the purposes of analysis, however, it is important that it is seen as a variable in the qualitative sense. Whether the unit needs more or less of it depends on the other three processes. The process of labour substitution simply means the replacement of one level of human capital for another – in both directions! Technological substitution implies the total replacement of a person by a machine. The concept of standardisation relates to the diversity of the tourism product. This is essentially a complexity/simplicity construct and is of vital importance in determining labour productivity. Fundamentally the proposition would be – the more complex the unit the less productive because of increased employment and higher human capital.

None of these ideas work independently of human capital. For example, the technological substitution of museum attendants by video cameras and security technicians may lower the residual employment level but it also may imply changes in human capital – different people with different skills or retraining. In the age of information technology those jobs which are data and information based, such as travel agent and reservations, may be vulnerable to technological substitution.

The assumption that productivity is a function of the relationship between the level of standardisation, the range of services provided, technological intervention and human capital has a common sense rationale to it. Surely greater standardisation would benefit productivity just as a wider range of services would adversely effect it. However, in the context of tourism, the relationship may be more complicated than that. For example, the range of services may have a marketing function irrespective of consumer preference. The range may be there to draw in the customer. In such circumstances, there are effects on productivity when consumers are attracted by a wide range of products and services but consume narrowly (the inherent problem of a la carte). This issue of the complexity of the product directly relates productivity to customer choice and implies that the level of choice is one of the parameters in assessing the potential productivity of a unit.

A complex unit with a wide range of services might require high human capital but a simple standardised unit might need lower levels of human capital. Clearly technological substitution and labour substitution are part of resolving this conundrum. It should not be assumed that such intervention necessarily means de-skilling. It could equally imply multi-skilling and even enhanced skilling. This last concern is important given that in some tourism occupations increased personal skill can increase sales. Such a phenomenon could explain the rare but occasional sightings of reverse employment effects (more people being employed when the price of labour rises) which occurs in tourism.

However, human capital is not simply a reactive variable; it can exert an influence. If machines are used or work processes simplified, then personal productivity can be increased. This is the straightforward 'efficiency' case where increased skill or simplification increases output. A skilled pizza maker, for example, will make more pizzas than a less skilled one. But, it could be argued that as output is determined by the chance element of customer demand, all you have done is increased potential productivity but not necessarily actual productivity. This may be true but there are two important ways to extend this line of thought. In the first instance, what we might be doing by extending personal productivity is minimising the residual level of employment. For example, if a museum attendant looks at a set of screens from which the whole museum can be surveyed, then clearly less attendants are needed for security. This worker's productivity, although detached from actual throughput, increased nevertheless because although the job remains one of watching a space the space is now bigger and although the worker is not more productive, the productivity of the whole unit has increased. In the second instance, a waiter who is trained in bar skills has enhanced human capital but this may not be reflected in output unless the waiter serves in the restaurant and the bar at the same time! What has happened here is an increase in the threshold of management's ability to substitute labour and therefore an increase in the capacity to match supply with demand. In both these senses increased human capital affects productivity.

Illustrating the Problem

Figure 3.1 is designed to illustrate the problem. It shows demand and supply movements over a five-day period in a hypothetical organisation that employs only two skills/occupations. In order to translate customer demand into a demand for labour forecast there has to be a productivity standard established. In this hypothetical case the ratio is one member of staff for two customers. In Figure 3.1: CD = customer demand; LD = forecast demand for labour based on 2:1 ratio; EL = a nominal level of full-time employment; SA = supply of skill A; SB = supply of skill B.

Figure 3.1 attempts to illustrate that matching supply to demand is two processes, namely, using a production standard to guide the manipulation of resources and finding an optimal employment level. Shortages affect quality and surpluses affect productivity, but it is not an exact science.

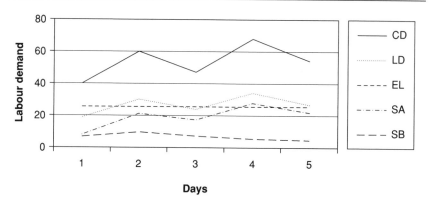

Figure 3.1 Supply and demand configuration

If labour productivity, in an operational sense, is a matter of matching labour supply to labour demand in the very short run, then two broad approaches suggest themselves. Use can be made of either mobility into and out of the external labour market, or internal labour resources can be manipulated. Adopting the external market approach implies letting labour turnover and recruitment processes act naturally to moderate the level of employment. There are various problems with this strategy. In the first place the mobility is disconnected from consumer demand variations and is in fact random mobility based on market and motivational factors. However, an unstable workforce, for whatever reason, does offer the opportunity for this approach not only to be adopted, but also to be successful. Its use is dependent upon the assumption of a labour market in constant surplus. At this point it is worth highlighting the established relationship between recruitment and labour turnover in organisations. As recruitment increases so does labour turnover as well. This is always true because the propensity to leave is highest when the employee has just joined and declines with increasing length of stay (Riley, 2000). This makes the use of the labour market as a manipulative tool a policy of sustained instability and that, in turn, has implications for the quality of products and services.

The internal approach tries to match supply to demand by using internal labour resources. One approach uses earnings flexibility such as increasing supply by overtime or through pay systems that automatically relate reward to performance such as tipping systems. A more complex internal approach advocates functional flexibility that has implications for training, multi-skilling programmes and strong internal labour markets. The idea of functional flexibility is to multi-skill staff so that they can be mobile across occupational boundaries. Common sense suggests that total substitutability, that is everyone able to do everyone else's job is unobtainable and probably undesirable as well, but how much flexibility is actually needed and is there an optimal? It is a question of the cross-utilisation of labour under conditions of variable demand but with fixed parameters (maximum capacity of the unit). The merits of functional flexibility are that they make better use of existing human resources and at the same time enhance job satisfaction and increase teamwork. However, there are obvious barriers to such policies most notably the need for employees to have an occupational identity. Notwithstanding such a barrier, it would be wrong to see functional flexibility as a total solution to the problem of labour productivity – it is a partial solution as the following example shows. The example uses the same hypothetical figures that were used to construct Figure 3.1.

If we assume a situation in which a unit workforce contains a number of jobs with different skills attached to them and that consumer demand is variable in the short run (i.e. hour, day) then, if there were no substitutability, the size of the workforce must equal the highest level of forecast demand for each job that occurs in the period. In these circumstances the residual minimum and the very maximum would be the same! But if 100% substitutability were the case then the residual minimum would be equal to the highest combined forecast demand across all jobs. Table 3.1 is an example of the principle and describes a hypothetical unit with two jobs over a five-day period in which demand fluctuates. Three further assumptions apply here, first, that the solution must be by internal resources; second, that transfer of staff between the days is ignored in the five-day planning period and third, that all demand will be met at the required level of quality

With no substitutability the minimum workforce size is 28 + 10 = 38. With 100% substitutability it becomes 28 + 6 = 34 a saving of over 10%. The minimum employment levels for each job, given substitutability, can be estimated from the maximum total demand and the maximum demand for the alternative job. Thus for Job A, the lower parameter would be 34 – 10 = 24 and for Job B it would be 34 – 28 = 6. In this

Table 3.1 Demand for skills

Day	1	2	3	4	5
Job/skill A	12	20	17	28	22
Job/skill B	7	10	7	6	5

example therefore, it follows that the optimum level of employment for Job A is between 28–24 and for Job B is between 10–6. The optimum combinations of A and B is within these parameters. The pairing 28–10 seems excessive and the minimum pairing of 24–6 fails on Day 4, so the answer is somewhere in between.

However, it is clear that at 34 there is still excess labour on four out of the five days. This is because the assumption made is that all demand will be met at the required level of quality. This is the juncture where notions of productivity actually meet ideas about quality. If we assume that, not having enough staff to meet demand adversely affects quality and we wish to maintain quality, then logically we will have to staff up to the highest level of demand. What this example is designed to show is that in some cases the decision to meet all demand creates excess supply even when you have total flexibility. This juncture, where productivity meets quality, is also where internal approaches meet external ones. The subtext here is that either management must accept fluctuating quality or accept fluctuating profits or, consciously decide not to meet all demand through internal resources. Brusco *et al.* (1998) take this analysis further and show the affect of cross utilisation on business performance.

Managerial Strategies

Labour flexibility and organisational change

Whilst it is possible to calculate the parameters of cross utilisation of labour, the implementation of a policy of labour flexibility implies a change in organisation culture and possibly structure. The demands of productivity have to be considered in an organisational context. Organisations have subsections and flexible labour implies that staff will not just use different skills but cross section boundaries as well. If staff are moving between sections of a unit then that redeployment requires both authority and agreement. The act has to be justified because it is an exchange of resources. The inherent danger is that it might become a matter of negotiation between supervisors or, a matter of 'favours' that require reciprocal action. It is to avoid these possibilities that the utilisation of multi-skilled labour has to be organised. It has to be a process so that the 'horse-trading' between sections is carried out without conflict. In other words, in constantly fluctuating circumstances, a degree of external manipulation is probably essential. In other words, to get the productivity from flexible labours needs teamwork and that is engendered by an organised system rather that an ad hoc one.

Substitution strategies

At first glance the above analysis of the problem may suggest that the only strategy on offer is one of substitution. In a sense, that is true. A pragmatic way of looking at the problem of labour productivity is simply to look at the substitution choices which crudely come down to four – capital for capital, capital for labour, labour for capital and labour for labour. However, motives have a role to play. What the analysis of the problem suggests is that productivity increases the need to be motivated not just by cost minimisation through cost substitution but also by 'responsiveness' strategies. Making resources responsive may be as helpful to the course of productivity as making them cheaper. This is an area where profitability and productivity come together.

Any resource can be regarded as responsive if it meets all or any combination of the following criteria:

- the degree to which it is more sustainable and less perishable (able to be stored);
- the degree to which it is has more than one purpose (flexible utility, e.g. multi-skilled labour);
- the degree to which it only incurs costs if used (e.g. casual labour); the degree to which it is substitutable (cooking skills for the equivalent bought in prepared food and vice versa).

Judging a resource by its responsiveness as distinct from its cost has the merit of focusing attention on the *performance of the resource*. This is not to imply that costs are secondary to efficiency nor that cost considerations are not a full part of valuing a resource but merely to suggest that with labour in tourism there is more to it than just labour cost.

Judging resources by responsiveness highlights a form of substitution that is not uncommon in sectors of the tourism industry namely, that of higher productivity for low labour costs. For example, the restaurant industry often, for a variety of reasons, uses more labour than it needs. It is not unknown for high standard food and beverage outlets to conceive good service as plenty of bodies, nor for restaurants to play part in ethnic enclave labour markets where the local labour market sustains an ethic community irrespective of growth and business performance. What is happening in both these cases is that productivity is deliberately being foregone for perfectly legitimate reasons (Wilson & Portes, 1980). A more serious case is where productivity, and particularly the contribution of capital input, is foregone simply because labour is relatively cheap. Alpert (1986) found evidence of this but also found sufficient contra-indicators to speculate that some American restaurant operators saw the productivity value of higher priced labour in that they could do one thing better than capital – sell.

Manpower system strategies

Given the inherent problem illustrated in Figure 3.1, it follows logically that a decrease of systematic information would assist the processes required. Such approaches are within the reach of large-scale operations. The basic requirements for such systems are the identification of those jobs that vary with demand and the setting of productivity standards for them. The system is only possible if consumer demand is forecast in the short-run (Baker & Riley, 1994). The system works as an aid to adjusting supply to anticipated demand but also has the merit of showing in retrospect both productivity and quality in the sense that highlighted shortages can be interpreted as problems of sustaining quality.

Productivity and Employment

One of the strongest arguments in favour of tourism development is that it provides employment. This aspect of its role needs to be qualified in the light of the proceeding arguments. As the demand for labour is direct, rates of employment should reasonably follow the growth of the demand for tourism. However, it should not be expected that increased tourism means increased employment. Two processes lie between the variables of growth and employment. These are first, the processes open to managers of adjusting supply to demand in the short run. Within units labour productivity can be increased through numerical, earnings and functional flexibility which implies a reduction in full time employment. Second, within a unit labour productivity is influenced by level of service. Levels of service can be manipulated in both directions but, at any given level of service, labour supply can be increased without increasing employment. However, there is a case for suggesting that one upward pressure on employment would be increased levels of service.

In the light of these arguments it is suggested that the relationship between tourism demand and employment would be better understood in terms of a net increase or decrease in the number of units in the industry. In other words, there should be a relationship between changes in the number of employing units and employment in tourism.

Conclusion

It was argued earlier that macro and micro studies of productivity work at different levels of abstraction. The principal culprit, it has been suggested, is the failure of macro studies to account for the phenomenon of short-term stochastic demand. As a result of this, macro-studies are difficult to interpret. In fact to get productivity in perspective it is necessary to broaden the view even beyond the scope of macro-studies. To appreciate the nature of productivity in tourism it is worth bringing into perspective elements of the industry's social, structural and technological environment. There are numerous sources of diversity within the industry that affect the level of awareness of productivity and the degree to which it is a priority. In motivational terms, the industry contains, across the range of sizes and standards, both the entrepreneurial desire for profit and the 'way of life' culture. Professionals and amateurs succeed and fail. In structural terms, the largely small unit structure exists along with a mixture of corporation, chains and independents. In technical terms, high technology and low technology exist side by side – global reservation systems exist alongside craft skills. In terms of regulation, all tourism industries are both regulated and market led.

In the light of such diversity it not too surprising that there are problems associated with the measurement of productivity. The rationale for focusing only on productivity is that, from the micro perspective it is a strong factor. Perhaps a pragmatic view might be that productivity is taken seriously only in a recession. Notwithstanding this, the arguments put forward here illustrate that it is essential for the sustainable growth of tourism that productivity is understood.

Chapter 4
Pay Determination

Introduction

The purpose of Chapter 4 is to create a framework by which the levels of pay and pay differentials in the tourism industry can be understood. Hard evidence presents difficulties because figures on pay are not often clearly distinguished in most national level statistics. However, what evidence is available, points in the same direction – towards relatively low pay. The analysis that follows makes three assumptions, first, that pay determination involves not just market competition but also intra-organisational processes. Second, that all the arguments on determination accumulate around the managerial decision to set the price of labour and third, that there is sufficient commonality between sectors of the tourism industry to make a conceptual framework possible. The theoretical perspective used to assist understanding is not comprehensive and is somewhat eclectic and selective and is only justified by the emphasis on the exploration of pay specifically in one industry; tourism. The intention is to take a general perspective on the industry and to identify where, within the structure and within motives of the participants, inflationary and deflationary pressures exist.

To an extent, the accusation of low pay is unfair because there is evidence to suggest that differentials exist and that some occupations and some organisations experience high remuneration. Notwithstanding such variation, the reputation of the industry is that of being one of low pay and, in terms of image of the industry as an employer, this is important. However, the assertion of low pay very much depends on perspective. From a subsistence level pay in tourism might not seem low. It is, in a sense, too easy to take a *'developed economy'* view as an overall perspective.

Level of Pay in the Industry: A Comparative Assessment

One way to make a general assessment of any industry's level of pay is to compare its main labour component with similar components in other sectors of the economy. Table 4.1 is extracted from statistics on average earning published by the International Labour Office in 1998. It uses the average earnings of hotel, retail and restaurant workers, as a rough proxy for tourism labour, and expresses the earnings of that category as a proportion of the average earnings in 1997 of all non-managerial, manual workers employed in all sectors except agriculture and fishing. The fact that agriculture and fisheries are singled out as exceptions is not without significance, as that category often shares a similarly low position on the pay ladder and is in some circumstances a source of tourism labour.

Nothing important can be read into Table 4.1 other than it gives a broad illustration that labour in tourism is relatively low paid – not once did it beat the average. To a degree, Table 4.1 substantiates the negative image of low pay. If there is some evidence of low pay in labour markets, which are similar, then it is reasonable to think that deflationary pressures are at work within the economics of that industry.

Table 4.1 Average earnings of tourism workers in selected countries, % of average earnings, 1997

Country	%
Costa Rica	86
Hong Kong	70
Israel	53
Mauritius	95
Mexico	69
New Zealand	84
Portugal	94
Singapore	84
Spain	75
Thailand	99
United Kingdom	65

Source: ILO Yearbook 1998.
Note: Non-managerial workers based on Categories 2–9 of the ISIC 2 classification or C–Q of the ISIC 3 classification. Hotel, retail and restaurant workers based on Category 6 or H respectively (there is an element of double countering involved). Figures are for men and women.

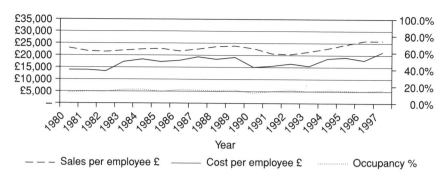

Figure 4.1 UK hotels: productivity sales and costs per employee, inflation adjusted

Figure 4.1 is evidence over time rather than cross-national but nevertheless points in the same direction. Based on a UK sample it shows the relationship between sales and labour costs over nearly two decades and by using inflation adjustments indicates that labour costs have been kept at roughly the same proportion of sales. It is evidence that either huge productivity gains have been made or that deflationary pressures operate within the system.

However, two pieces of evidence are far from the complete picture and an understanding of tourism employment requires a more substantial grasp of how pay, in the tourism industry, is determined. In this respect the task is to try to explain both the level of pay and the pay differentials.

Pay Determination: Some Theoretical Considerations

By way of background, a brief outline of some useful theoretical perspectives would be helpful. These perspectives come from several different directions namely, individual attributes, job attributes, organisational attributes and industrial structure, but all seek to explain both levels of pay and differentials. They should be seen as a set of integrated explanations. What must be borne in mind however is that levels of pay in one economic sector, such as tourism, can not be separated from the market's influence on all sectors. In other words, explanations of levels of pay are explanations of relative pay.

The theoretical perspectives applied here are built around five separate areas, these are:

• The level of skill and the ease with which skills can be learnt.

- The attractiveness of the jobs.
- Industrial structure.
- The concept of the internal labour market.
- The affect on management of demand uncertainty.

These areas are integrated by the theoretical ideas that attach to them. Each will be explored before being applied to tourism.

Skills, Job Attributes and Markets

An obvious place to start is with job attributes simply because they link directly to characteristics of the labour market through the type of skills they demand. Add to this the fact that the actual vehicle for pay determination will be the forces of supply and demand within the labour market then the route to understanding of pay distribution is through factors that affect market mechanisms of distributing skills. In simple terms, this means identifying factors that explain the size and segmentation of the labour market and the speed with which supply and demand interact therein. One way of conceiving these factors is to look at the relationship between, on the one hand, job attributes or characteristics and on the other, market features. Table 4.2 displays four job attributes and the market affect they engender. Two concepts are particularly important in the job attribute-market characteristic relationship. First, human capital, which is the amount of education and experience required by a job and second, skill specificity, which refers to the degree to which the skills of the job are unique to the organisation. In Table 4.2 the direction is, in each case, towards a greater amount and the argument is that the reverse direction would produce the reverse affects.

Interpreting Table 4.2, if a job requires high levels of education and skills which are almost unique to the employing organisation, then the external labour market would be small and supply and demand would be slow to respond to changes in the levels of pay. Similarly, if the output of a job could be accurately measured then selection could be more precise which may decrease the market size but let differentials reflect competition. Seen in this light, perhaps the most significant influence of job attributes is that it prescribes levels of skill. The relationship between skill and pay follows from the capacity of skill to determine the size of the labour market the employer recruits from. The lower the level of skill required the larger the labour market will be, and, in line with human capital theory, the greater the skill the smaller the market. In addition, skill creates pay differentials both between industries and between occupations within an

Table 4.2 Linking job and labour market characteristics

Job characteristic	Direction	Labour market character
Input of human capital (education + experience)	The greater	• Smaller market • Slow response to changes in supply or demand
Specificity of skills	The greater uniqueness of skills to the organisation	• Smaller market • Slow response to changes in supply and demand
Individual qualities and attributes count	The greater	• Larger market • Faster response to changes in supply and demand • Wide differentials for the same job
The ease of measuring the performance output	The greater	• Wide differentials for the same job

organisation. Differentials represent rewards for skills acquired and simultaneously provide an incentive for people to learn the skills.

Human capital is a concept that can apply to jobs but in theoretical terms is generally applied to individuals. Human capital theory suggests that the pay of an individual is primarily attributable to individual attributes such as education, experience in the job and accumulated experience in the labour market. It follows logically therefore that rewards to those similarly endowed would be the same across industries and organisations. In other words, levels and differentials are explainable by differences in amounts of skill and knowledge. By this argument those who invest in education should earn more than those who do not. Similarly, the more experienced worker will earn more than the less experienced one. Putting this argument in terms of labour market size, human capital theories suggest that it is likely that those with high levels of human capital will inhabit relatively small labour markets. The crux of this argument is that the returns to those with similar levels of human capital would be the same across industrial and organisational boundaries.

Skills, Job Attributes and Individual Attributes

From Adam Smith onwards the attractiveness of a job has been accepted as having an influence on the reward it carries. There are two aspects of this argument: first, that increasing attractiveness itself makes the labour market larger (subject to human capital constraints) and second, where personality attributes is a selection criterion, it combines with attractiveness to produce both low pay and pay differentials between people in the same occupation. This second argument, that personality and personal attributes count, can be taken inside the organisation to produce an explanation for differentials. Stinchcombe (1963) suggests that pay differentials can be explained by differentiating jobs in terms of whether they are 'talent additive' or 'talent complementary'. In the latter case, the individual's output is disproportionately higher and therefore attracts a higher rate of pay.

One problem always attaches itself to the attractiveness arguments and that is why some jobs, which are low paid, are found attractive and recruit from a larger labour market thus deflating the level of pay. The commonest explanations involve compensatory factors such as the intrinsic attributes of the job or some extrinsic benefit other than pay. Two compensatory factors are particularly important – the opportunity to learn and the convenience of working hours.

Learning could be part of the attraction of a job. Rosen (1972) points out that the capacity of a job to teach has a downward affect on the rate of pay. He argues that certain jobs are seen as opportunities to learn and therefore employers assume short tenure and offer a rate that represents the role the job is playing in a recognised career progression. He suggests that, in theory, there is a virtual market wage which is above the actual market rate and which represents the rate firms would have to pay if they recruited fully-trained and experienced people into vacancies. By not doing that, employers forego productivity in favour of lower labour costs. It is not difficult to speculate that, in an industry where skills are easy to learn and inter-firm mobility relatively accessible, those employers will assume short tenure and pay accordingly. It is a seductive argument. This notion highlights two further aspects of jobs; first, that jobs can exist in sequences within organisations and across organisations and therefore, the rate of pay is linked to other jobs within the organisation and in the marketplace. Second, that the jobs and pay are surrounded by many other motivations.

One such motivation may be the desire to work social hours whereby leisure time is shared with the general population. If a market existed for the same set of skill but was segmented by social and unsocial hours the effect may be to cause mobility in the direction of the social hours market.

Industrial Structure: Structural and Organisational Factors

Explanations for the levels of pay have to involve the structure of the industry and the size and number of organisations that make up its labour market. The relationship between structural-organisational factors and pay is through the influence of these factors on mobility and career opportunity. In other words, structure is an enabling factor which either encourages or discourages job change, location change and the seeking of advancement. The capacity of any industry to provide opportunities is dependent on its size and structure characteristics. The ability to provide competitive conditions that engender mobility between jobs and firms in the market has a determining affect on pay levels.

The context of job and career opportunity is not just a matter of bureaucratic structures; the labour market has an important role. The interplay of structure and market is crucial to understanding how opportunity affects pay. Industrial structure is the context in which the influence of competition and bureaucratic imperatives operate on pay levels, differentials and mobility patterns, of which career ladders are one such pattern. Essentially the structural arguments involve five related components, which are, size of operating units, the geographical dispersion of those units, the degree of specialisation, the ownership structure of the units and managerial strategies.

The first two work together to determine employment concentrations, that is, whether employees are grouped in large numbers in close proximity or dispersed in smaller groupings. In terms of pay, there are three important variables; size of company, size of plant or unit size and geographical dispersion. Research suggests that size of company has the greater influence on the rate of pay. One argument to support this assertion is that large companies, because of the opportunities for advancement they offer, attract better workers who are more productive (Evans & Leighton, 1989).

If the size variable is taken together with the degree of functional specialisation within the organisation then this simultaneously forms the opportunity structure. It creates hierarchical levels and specialisms with pay differentials acting as an incentive to all forms of mobility. This would suggest that the same organisational structure would produce an identical pay structure but this is unlikely. One of the major theoretical tenets of organisational behaviour, contingency theory, argues that there is no single effective organisation structure and there is a constant realignment of the fit between the actual structure and the demands of structural factors such as size and technological change. One outcome of this is that there are differences in the importance allotted to the same job in different organisations. This creates market pay differentials that have no market explanation as they are conceived entirely for intra-organisational purposes.

Women's Work?

A high proportion of women in an occupation is often advocated as an explanation for low pay. Attached to this idea are a bundle of issues to do with attachment to the labour market and discrimination. In the context of this analysis, possibly a more useful argument is that women are low-paid because they work in low paid-jobs. The economic system produces low paid jobs irrespective of who does them. The fact that high proportions of occupants of such jobs are women does not cause the level of pay. It is the reverse of the discrimination argument, and it points the finger at the nature of jobs themselves (Murgatroyd, 1982).

Internal Labour Markets

Whilst it goes without saying that management has the authority to set pay rates their influence on pay determination goes beyond this right. If it is accepted that pay is determined by the labour market, then the degree to which the market itself is the actual agent is matter of managerial choice. Management can choose how far they let the market, as against their own agency, set pay levels. In fact, it is a structural issue. The salient concept here is that of the internal labour market (ILM). The idea of an ILM is that it is an alternative to the external labour market (ELM). In other words, management has a choice as to how far they let the ELM influence their pay rates because it is possible for them to create their own internal rules. These rules would cover how skills are to be distributed within the organisation and by what pay differentials jobs are to be differentiated. The key elements of such an internal market are rules about promotion criteria, training opportunities, pay differentials, job evaluation and above all about which jobs are 'open' to the ELM and which are not. This control of the ELM by designated 'ports of entry' is the defining feature of an internal labour market. The importance of this concept to our understanding of pay cannot be overstated. Riley

(1996) introduced the concept of the weak and strong ILM. In the former the influence of the ELM is strong so that the internal pay rate accords with the market rate and organisations experience high labour turnover. In the case of the strong ILM, jobs and rates of pay are internally valued and therefore, to an extent, detached from the market. The original advocates of internal labour market theory, Doeringer and Piore (1971), argue that the rationale for an ILM is the degree of specificity of skills required by the organisation. The more unique the skills the greater is the incentive to avoid the external market and try to maintain a stable workforce. Where skills are not unique and can be obtained in the ELM there would be little incentive to erect an ILM. However, modern ideas about 'quality' have given the rationale for a strong ILM another impetus. If quality of service requires continuity of employment then structural devices such as a strong ILM are seen as one way to ensure a stable workforce. If the organisation is unionised then a strong ILM is automatic, the only difference being that its architecture will be the outcome of negotiation rather than management design.

Demand Uncertainty

The demand for labour can be characterised into direct and indirect. In the former case workers are demanded for what they can produce and, in such circumstances, the demand curve for labour tracks the level of demand by consumers. This is another way of saying that employment levels follow sales. This is not the case where demand is indirect and derived from the productivity of machines. In these circumstances employment levels are, to an extent, unhinged from consumer demand. This difference is important and is especially so when firms employing workers of the first type are faced with uncertain consumer demand. The basic argument here is that when demand is variable in the short run then management needs to have employment flexibility, which in turn breeds short-term policies. This means policies that do not reward tenure. In such circumstances experience is expendable. If, in addition, the industry also works on low profit margins then the affect is amplified. This is a deflationary influence on the level of pay.

Minimum Wage Regulation

Much of the literature on the minimum wage has as its main theme the question of whether or not minimum wage regulation reduces employment. The empirical evidence on this point comes mainly from

America and is contradictory and inconclusive (Card & Krueger, 1995). In relation to the level of pay, the key question is whether a base level minimum causes a 'knock-on effect'. This takes the form of first, rates rising above the minimum as the conditions of competition change. Second, differentials in the same organisation above the base rate rise as a consequence. Third, rates of pay in jobs which are not covered by the regulation but which are close in skill and proximity terms come under pressure to rise. The conditions of competition and extent of unionisation come into play in this issue. Usually workers covered by minimum wage regulation do not have the negotiating power to force rates to rise, so the knock-on effect, if it happens, is due to some market shortage. Minimum wages could have the effect of enlarging the market by bringing people who are not working back into employment.

The purpose of the above discussion has been to introduce some theoretical ideas that may assist in the understanding of pay in tourism. In looking at the tourism industry the analysis that follows seeks to identify inflationary and deflationary pressures.

Pay Determination in the Tourism Industry

Skill and attractiveness

The principal issue that has to be faced in this respect is the *combined* effects of attractiveness and easily acquired skills. Although tourism occupations have a number of attractive features such as glamour, travel, variety, and people orientation, the actual source of attractiveness is immaterial with one exception. Attractiveness influences pay through two processes, the first concerns its affect in increasing the size of the labour market and the second is concerned with that part of attractiveness based on the desire for learning. These influences draw the same response from management – that of offering lower pay. When, as in most tourism occupations, attractiveness is considered against a background of relatively low skills that can be acquired easily, then, the affect of these two processes is amplified. These processes attach a cost to an occupation which is borne by the worker. Mobility can be seen to 'oil' these processes.

Normally workers can take advantage of organisation-specific human capital to improve earnings by moving to organisations with such capital and then staying on to take advantage of the organisation's need to keep them for their acquired specific skills (Mincer & Jovanovic, 1981). This is unlikely to be the case with tourism employment for two reasons. First, due to employers offering rates of pay which accept that job tenure will be short because of the learning and then advancement process. The skill framework advocated by Riley (1991) suggests that this possibility is the case in tourism. This conceptual framework argues that, in the case of hotel labour markets, workers collect skills through mobility between units of different classes and that the industry structure both facilitates and encourages this. Second, although there are skills which are organisation specific, these too can be acquired quickly, and therefore only a limited monetary advantage accrues to the individual. This implies a competitive market based on small increments where workers trade-off skill acquisition for low pay. The sustainability of such a market depends on the capacity of the industry to recruit in a fairly large market, and provide both on-the-job training and opportunities for advancement. A further consequence of the relative ease of access to skills and knowledge is that productivity is not strongly related to job tenure. When to this is added the notion of productivity being demand-led then, there is little incentive to reward long tenure that has a deflationary influence on levels of pay.

Skill and structure

If, to the relationship between accumulating skills and knowledge and mobility, is added the context of industrial structure then it is possible to model this relationship more securely. A model of skill, structure and mobility aids our understanding of pay. The thrust of this model is that skill and structure 'conspire' to engender labour mobility, particularly inter-organisational mobility that in turn has a deflationary affect on pay.

The assumptions of such a proposition are founded on the structure of the industry displaying a particular constellation of characteristics, which are:

(1) That, irrespective of ownership, the structure of the industry consists of small operating units operating in local markets. Superimposed on this small unit structure is an ownership structure that combines large companies and large chains operating in wider markets with independent operators.
(2) The small size of the operating unit means that hierarchies will be fairly flat which suggests limited opportunities for advancement within the unit.
(3) Every operating unit has a finite limit on how much it can teach. Once the skills and knowledge have been learnt further development requires mobility to another establishment.

(4) Operating units are organised through functional specialisation. This carries the risk of the phenomenon of occupational rigidity whereby people have to change employer to change skills. In such cases where there are barriers for employees who wish to move to other jobs within the unit, mobility between units or employers becomes a ready option. The presence of functional flexibility would offset this influence.

(5) It is the case that, even skills and knowledge that are specific to a unit of a company can be acquired reasonably quickly.

(6) Crucially, that skills and knowledge are transferable between units and employers.

(7) That the skills and knowledge of the industry are such that labour 'spills over' into other labour markets.

The behavioural characteristic associated with this model is high levels of labour turnover. This phenomenon is often perceived as pathological but the logic of this particular model suggests that, in terms of constantly renewing skills in the industry, it may, in part, be beneficial.

The argument here is that, if these factors pertain then, they not only enable but also encourage labour mobility. It is not suggested that the entire tourism industry displays the above structural characteristics merely, that in many sectors of the industry, this is the case. Although it is not possible to regard all tourism occupations as belonging to one single labour market, it is argued that all segmented labour markets share the structure of the industry and are therefore open to its influence. To a large extent, different parts of the tourism industry have separate occupational labour markets for example; waiters inhabit different sections of the secondary labour market from coach drivers. However, some overlap is possible, for example hotel receptionists and travel agent clerks might inhabit the same market. Yet, when the notion of transferable skills is superimposed on to segmented markets one important factor emerges which is, that the secondary labour market can be seen as a dual market separated by social and unsocial hours of work. A hotel receptionist can become an airline passenger agent but also a dentist's receptionist – a hotel food and beverage manager can become an industrial catering manager. The affect of this market structure is dependent on the value contained in the exchange of hours for pay. If the differential is small then the value of working social hours rises. In such circumstances, the rate of mobility out of tourism employment would increase. The argument here is that the differential between occupations sharing skills, but with differential hours of work patterns is a key factor in determining the pay of those in unsocial hours occupations.

Essentially the case for the influence of industrial structure involves two related components, which are, size of operating units and the geographical dispersion of those units. These components work together to determine employment concentrations. In this respect, the tourism industry is characterised by a dual structure with, on the one hand, many examples of high employment density, such as in resorts, airports and large organisations and on the other, geographically-fragmented small concentrations such as, hotels, restaurants, visitor attraction centres, car hire offices. One additional aspect of structure impinges on size and dispersion and that is where ownership is concentrated in large organisations but the dispersion of staff is fragmented. In these circumstances management have a choice either to manage all staff in the same way or allow for local circumstances. What usually arbitrates this decision is the degree of job uniformity between the operating units. If exactly the same job is carried out in widely dispersed locations then it might be rational to manage them in the same way and give them identical employment conditions. What is important however is that industrial structure is the context in which the influence of competition and bureaucratic imperatives operate on pay levels and differentials.

What distinguishes some sectors of the industry from conformity to the model is the structural device they use to offset its effects. This 'device' is the adoption of a strong internal market.

Internal labour markets

Although there is strong evidence that hotels, irrespective of size or ownership, tend to operate weak internal labour markets (Simms *et al.*, 1988; Riley *et al.*, 2000) other sectors, such as airlines, have strong internal markets. It might be surprising to some that even large hotel chains appear to have weak internal markets but, notwithstanding corporate ownership, the hotels themselves live in local labour markets and seek the advantages from such local markets. In theoretical terms, the most powerful motivation for setting up a strong internal market is skill specificity and it could be argued that airlines and tour operators contain some fairly unique skills. However, a more likely explanation lies in the need to manage large numbers of people concentrated in one location. These circumstances push management towards a bureaucratic solution involving clear hiring standards, formal promotion criteria, restricted ports of entry and established pay differentials between jobs. In other words, internal market mechanisms are based on managerial criteria not external market forces. One particular feature of such a bureaucratic approach, the existence of a job evaluation scheme, is confirmation of a strong internal market. Once pay is set by internal criteria then, to an extent, the influence of the external market is curtailed. One behavioural consequence of such a market is a stable workforce, that is, low labour turnover. Trade unions could be part of that strong internal market in which case the negotiation process influences the pay differentials set through job evaluation. The essential argument here is that strong internal labour markets, whether negotiated with unions or not, exert an inflationary pressure because they reward tenure and reduce competition.

Demand uncertainty

Whilst it is true that for large parts of the tourism industry consumer demand is seasonal, the arguments concerning uncertainty go beyond this notion of variable, but reasonably predictable, demand pattern. Riley *et al.* (2000), in arguing a case for economic determinism in human resource management practice, puts forward two aspects of the same argument. First, that, short-term fluctuations in demand determine labour productivity. Managers seek to control labour costs by manipulating supply through numerical and earnings flexibility. Second, and very much related, is the suggestion that constant daily concern to match supply with fluctuating demand leads to a short-term 'mentality' which, in real terms, means 'leave it to the market to set the rates of pay'.

Fundamentally, the idea is that, given the constant need for short-term variations in supply, management set up weak internal labour markets so that recruitment and labour turnover fluctuations can help them to match supply with demand. Earnings variation in the form of overtime or flexible pay systems, such as tipping and its variants, further extends the possibilities for controlling labour supply. What is important here is that such short-term devices exert a deflationary pressure on pay when the market is plentiful. Gowler and Legge (1970) have argued convincingly that pay systems, of which tipping would be an example relate pay and performance so directly as to absorb the conflict which occurs when supply and demand are temporally mismatched. In other words, when the workload is suddenly increased the extra effort is paid for quickly by the gratuity system. Feelings of resentment about having to work harder are ameliorated by the fairly instant return. People, who work under this kind of pay system, simply get used to fluctuations in workload and this feeling is constantly being re-enforced by the variation in earnings. In this sense, pay systems can be considered to be conflict prevention mechanisms. They have the effect of focusing the worker's attention on earnings as against basic pay which, in aggregate terms, probably acts as a deflationary pressure.

One interesting aspect of demand uncertainty is the fact that measures to manipulate labour supply are incorporated into union agreements (Riley, 1993b). This is testimony to the influence of the short-term economic imperatives that drive tourism operations. Management negotiates some form of capacity to regularly adjust labour supply so that, even within a strong internal labour market, a degree of flexibility is recognised as being essential. It is likely that the influence of this type of agreement will fall on employment numbers or earnings rather than pay levels. In other words, such agreements operate either through a reserve pool of labour or through flexible working time that may, in turn, alter earnings. In this context statutory minimum wages or negotiated base rates are merely a platform on which the manipulation takes place (Alpert, 1986).

Given that demand uncertainty plays a key role in asserting the need for labour cost control, this argument needs to be broadened to include the perspective of business strategy. Tourism pricing tends to be forward-pricing based on seasons and with adjustments made on a discounting basis. This contrasts with the short-term pricing of labour that is made on a contingent basis. On the assumption that consumer prices are resistant to being lowered all the burden of adjustment falls on labour. This is a deflationary pressure on pay.

Motives, Satisfactions and Customers

Any exploration of the attractiveness of tourism has to confront not just the fact of low pay but that it is tolerated and can even exist alongside expressions of reasonably high job satisfaction. Sources of job satisfaction are not the prime issue. Here what matters is the role which pay plays in evaluation of a job. The basic question that needs to be addressed is why workers, by their market behaviour, appear to be complicit in an outcome which, at least in economic terms, is not in their interests. Some answers come from the nature of service work itself. The literature suggests that workers recognise intrinsic value in service work, particularly its variety, its scope for autonomy, and value the small working groups in which it is normally conducted and, as a consequence of this, are prepared to seek satisfaction from such attributes; despite low pay. This may be a rationalisation based on perceived life-chances but there is evidence of loyalty to particular sectors of the tourism industry if not to particular employers and also of a distinct feeling of 'not factory' in their expectations.

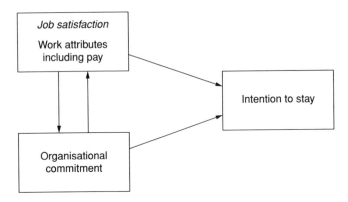

Figure 4.2 Relationship between job satisfaction commitment and
labour turnover

In considering the plight of low paid workers there are two areas to
be explored – how pay satisfaction and levels of job satisfaction are
related to each other and by what means are pay levels self-assessed.

From the perspective of established models that link satisfaction
to organisational commitment and labour turnover, pay is part of satisfaction (Price & Mueller, 1981). However, there is evidence that some
categories of low paid worker, in their evaluation of their lot, separate
pay from aspects of the job and are thus able to maintain dissatisfaction
with pay and high job satisfaction (Riley *et al.*, 1998). Figure 4.2 shows
the normal relationship between job satisfaction commitment and labour
turnover in which pay is part of satisfaction.

If pay is part of satisfaction as Figure 4.2 suggests then incidences of
low pay and high job satisfaction are hard to explain. One clue comes
from the consistent finding that lower paid workers express higher satisfaction with pay than higher paid workers (Brown & McIntosh, 1998). The
explanation for this relies not on a split of pay from job satisfaction but
that after a certain point pay becomes less important to satisfaction and
hence the higher paid consider other aspect more salient than pay. The
idea behind this is that of 'target earnings'. Once these earnings are
reached other job attributes take over. Because target earnings are subjectively determined they are hard to measure and research often adopts
proxy measures such as expected earnings (Drakopoulos & Theodossiou,
1997). Despite this, there is a degree of substance to the idea that satisfaction with pay is influenced by aspiration. An alternative explanation
is expressed in Figure 4.3.

Figure 4.3 Pay separated from job satisfaction

Figure 4.3 illustrates the case often found in service occupations where pay is separated from satisfaction.

Explanations as to how this separation occurs rest largely on the notion of 'trading off' attributes (Shapira, 1981). There is insufficient evidence to identify the actual process. In the case of tourism, this separation may be engendered by the locus of commitment being other than the paying employer. The transferability of skills means that the commitment and loyalty aspect of the model can be directed at the industry as a whole rather than any particular employer. This also suggests a deflationary pressure through the medium of inter-firm mobility.

Here again we return to the importance of mobility. If commitment is not to employer but to the industrial sector or occupation then the question arises as to the nature of pay referents. Pay satisfaction is influenced through comparisons and the identity of pay referents is a crucial part of understanding workers' attitudes to their pay. Making invidious comparisons may be a bargaining ploy but it is always constrained by pragmatism. The 'people like us' principle usually applies. If comparisons are made on the criterion of similar skills then the process of referent selection becomes a deflationary influence in itself. Expected earnings, the guiding star of pay satisfaction can be depressed to industrial sector norms that are simply re-enforced by mobility. In this way, pay in tourism, despite being relatively low, may not be considered as such by recipients.

Against these kind of models must be set the notion of satisfaction with influence on pay determination. Pay satisfaction and bargaining power are strongly related in the industrial relations literature. This is brought out strongly where pay satisfaction is studied within unionised environments (Capelli & Sherer, 1988). Tourism workers are like any other type of worker – they would like an influence on their level of pay. The fact that this is not often the case is due to structural factors and the nature of service work. One consequence of the nature of service work is that the variety of tasks and diversity between the same occupation that are a common feature of the industry is itself problematic to pay regulation in a fundamental way. Where output cannot be directly measured and the work effort is reliant on contingency, job regulation and valuation is difficult. This is the problem that lies at the heart of job evaluation and unionisation. In a sense, the problem of regulating job diversity is the same for job evaluation and union recruitment strategy – they share the same destiny.

Having pointed the finger at mobility as a source of downward pressure on pay it is important to consider the role of continuity of employment and its relationship to quality. It is possible to suggest that consumer demand for quality is an upward pressure on rates of pay. The argument being that, if quality means continuity of service then the need to retain staff would not just lead to competitive pressures but also the setting up of strong internal labour markets which reward tenure. The notion that retention is simply a matter of competitive rates of pay is a common managerial delusion but is one which hotel managers, for one, do not appear to suffer from (Riley, 1990a).

High Pay and Differentials

The analysis above has highlighted, what appear to be mainly deflationary pressures on the level of pay. Three dominant factors emerge, which are, recruiting in large labour markets, high levels of mobility and the propensity, in some areas, to have weak internal labour markets. None of this, however, can account for the fact that by any standards, there are many occupations and many organisations in the tourism industry that are associated with high pay. Taking size and profitability variables as given, four additional factors might account for such differentials.

First, the case where high-level skills are not exclusive to the industry. In other words, where non-related skills such as business or specialist skills are needed by the industry the incumbents of occupations are connected to a wider primary labour market. This wider market may have conditions of competition that raise pay above tourism industry norms. Second, even in the absence of a strong internal labour market certain highly-skilled tourism occupation could be well paid because of market forces. Highly-skilled chefs may be an example. Third, organisations may value the same role differentially and this may be reflected in pay differentials in the same job. In a sense, this argument goes against the idea of a dominant external labour market where management passively accept the pay rates dictated by the market. What it really suggests is that, even when faced with an abundant supply, managers are not passive and undiscriminating. Finally, in an industry where, in some occupations, personality is demanded for itself, this can create uniqueness that raises pay through market scarcity. The notion of individuals adding value beyond their output is not difficult to associate with tourism. Not included in these four factors however, is the influence of collective bargaining in unionised circumstances.

Intermediate Conceptual Frameworks

The purpose of the above analysis had been to pull together a template – a way of seeing levels of pay in the tourism industry. The theoretical framework has been selective and the analysis hampered by lack of empirical studies but nevertheless, the analysis is based on observed behavioural patterns and on general economic evidence. What has emerged is, in fact three templates each of which converges on managerial decision-making and on worker decision-making. The first template related to the role of job attributes, Figure 4.4 outlines the contribution of the nature of job attributes.

The key issues are that the nature of the jobs are such that they encourage management to assume short tenure and therefore not to reward seniority or to pay for learning.

The second template is concerned with the role of industrial structure where a complex set of inter-related variables exert influence on both managerial and worker psychology. Figure 4.5 outlines the contribution of industrial structure.

The key issue here is the encouragement of mobility by structure with its knock-on effect on pay. The conclusion that earnings variation leads to people overlooking the terms of their basic pay comes from the industrial relations and pays systems literatures. Put simply, if a person is in a position where they have to regularly add up the components of their earnings and compare them with, say, those of the previous week, they might forget that the starting point is rather low. The final template

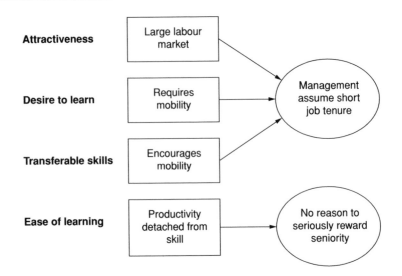

Figure 4.4 The contribution of job attributes

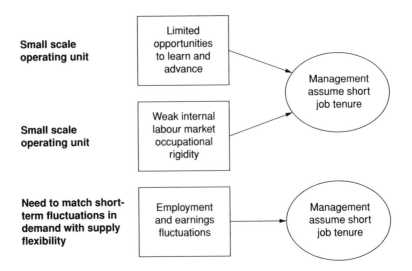

Figure 4.5 The contribution of structure and economics

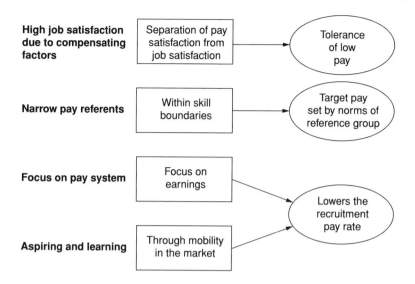

Figure 4.6 Contribution of psychological issues

builds upon the previous two and focuses exclusively on worker psychology. Figure 4.6 looks at the process which draws together the primary influences on the worker's perspective.

Figure 4.6 displays the network of psychological causal paths that lower expectations through realistic comparisons and increase the tolerance of low pay. 'Realistic low aspiration' is a self fulfilling promise but one that is encouraged by the system.

The Big Picture

The templates described above can be seen as intermediate constructions in the formation of an overall perspective. In attempting to describe a conceptual framework for understanding pay three ideas have emerged as being crucial to its construction. These are, first, that most of the pressures identified in the analysis were deflationary. The only strong inflationary forces identified were that of a consumer desire for quality working its way into a need for a stable workforce, unionism and a genuine shortage in the market for which the importation of skill is not an option. Second, that pay referents may be circumscribed by pragmatic considerations. If, the circumstantial evidence (more fully discussed in Chapter 5) suggesting that occupational or industrial communities (Salaman, 1974) exist within the tourism workforce is assumed, then a case must exist for low pay being maintained by deflationary norms shared by both workers and managers in the industry. If pay referents are confined to sector cultures – 'being a hotel worker', being an 'airline worker' etc, then pay levels may be maintained by the assumptions of all people working in those sectors. In other words, the forces that determine pay are embedded in the industrial cultures of tourism sectors that, in turn, share as many similar features as they have common job attributes and structures. Third, that there exists, for most workers a social hours alternative market. It is this feature that creates the outflow from the industry that the whole cycle of mobility, to an extent, depends upon. The likelihood is that it too is a deflationary pressure but is a seriously under-researched area and interpretation cannot be conclusive.

Conclusion

This analysis has progressed through three levels of abstraction. It began with evidence of the influence of job attributes, industrial structure and pay satisfaction which were developed into three templates. The larger perspectives draw upon this as explanations for a conclusion of strong deflationary pressures secured within an industrial culture.

Chapter 5
The Nature of Service Labour

Introduction

Although tourism employment embraces a wide range of occupations that appear, at one level, to have nothing in common, on closer inspection however, an important degree of commonality can be detected. There are underlying common characteristics across jobs with different titles and between jobs in different sectors. The importance of understanding this commonality lies first, in that it enables analysis to unpack the sweeping generalisations that are so often used to describe the industry, such a *'service industry'* and *'service workers'*. These kinds of labels have a macro utility but convey inaccurate information. Second, and more importantly, policy makers both at governmental and organisational levels have, of necessity, to make generalised assumptions and apply generic strategies to the diverse working population. These policy makers either assume a commonality or assume that differences do not matter. The argument is that it is helpful at all levels of analysis to understand what the numerous occupations, which populate the tourism industry, actually share. Third, by understanding the commonality the real sources of differentiation can be recognized and appreciated. Strange bedfellows may not look so strange on closer inspection.

Nature of Tourism Work

The source of this commonality with tourism employment lies in the nature of the work itself. The nature of the work affects behaviour at work and therefore what is shared by different occupations would produce similar behaviour and shared experience. What is being examined here is the determining affect of work, that is the tasks prescribed by the job, on behaviour. It is, in attributional terms, a situational perspective on work. What affects, both behavioural and psychological, stem from doing a particular type of work? This analysis assumes a socio-technical perspective, that is, to put it simply; we do things because the job tells us to! Jobs contain properties that give the incumbents of those jobs certain priorities. For example, waiting at table can be many things but it cannot be slow; a certain speed imperative is always there. All this is not a denial of human agency and individual differences it is simply a device to tease out the commonality within the obvious diversity.

Social-Psychological Processes

The analysis that follows examines some frequently-occurring attributes of tourism work in terms of what they mean for three universal concepts that are intrinsic to the very notion of work itself. The concepts under scrutiny are the psychological contract (sometimes known as the labour contract), the process of attitude formation and re-enforcement and personal strategies for coping with work.

The psychological contract

The psychological labour contract is a fundamental part of all employment relationships (Rousseau, 1995). In its simplest conception it has two principal dimensions which are, effort–reward (the so-called effort-bargain) and obedience–discipline (authority relations). How much effort do I put in for the expected reward? Which orders do I obey? How conditional is my willingness? How much discipline will I accept? These are the trade-offs and balances that form the heart of the contract – they are universal to every employment relationship. However, they exist for the most part at a covert level, in the realm of private thought rather than explicit behaviour. Their existence in private thought is in the form of assumptions about what is expected and what is acceptable and normal. It is a matter of psychological exchange but one in which the substance of the exchange is always indeterminate and subjective (Riley, 1996). Being covert, indeterminate and subjective the contract is always imprecise and that being so, gives it the potential for conflict. It is this aspect that gives it its prominence in the industrial relations literature (Hyman & Brough, 1975).

The original bargain is struck at the selection interview where the outcome is always imprecise. The employer is buying an unspecified potential and an unknown degree of willingness, the employee is taking on an indeterminate amount of work and an unspecified degree of discipline.

Like anything that is imprecise, it is open to misinterpretation and is, as is any agreement, potentially unstable. What keeps a psychological contract stable is the mutuality of the assumptions that lie behind it. As the relationship progresses the contract is adjusted until both parties feel comfortable with the implied mutual expectations. The level of the agreement is covert – founded on assumptions. What is important to the arguments here is that whilst the contract is always imprecise there are *degrees of imprecision which are determined by the nature of the work/technological process in which the job exists.* In other words, some jobs make for very imprecise labour contracts and others attract more precise contracts, the determinant of both is the nature of the job itself and to what degree it allows management to apply formal controls. The more precisely the job can be defined then the easier it becomes for management to apply formal control processes. It is this aspect of imprecise definition of jobs that has to be carried into the analysis of tourism employment.

Occupational community and attitude re-enforcement

There is nothing ostensibly wrong with a group of workers sharing the same occupational values; it is often good for morale and teamwork. A certain complexity arises, however, when those workers are isolated from the general population. The principle at stake here is called the 'isolation-integration principle' and it emphasizes how such work values can be reinforced or diluted by the degree to which the workforce is integrated in the wider local society. If the workforce is by some means isolated from the wider society, then it is likely that their values of work will be reinforced by life outside work *then brought back to work as an attitude.* The form of isolation may be geographical or related to unsocial hours but essentially it is immaterial. What matters is that the workforce lacks contact with the general population. By contrast, the integration argument suggests that when workers go home and socialize with workers from other industries, 'talking shop' is less likely and grumbles are disarmed by comparisons. In these circumstances, what happens at work stays at work. In this sense it is process.

Individual strategies for coping with the demands of the job

Every job has to be 'coped with'. The factory worker has to cope with routine and monotony just as the 'front-end' service worker has to cope with the 'hassle' of constant customer demands. For example, getting a

coach load of tourists to meet their cruise ship on time is a case of interdependent deadlines. There is potential friction here that has to be coped
with. In all these cases personal strategies are involved.

Each of these concepts is a process of some kind. It is now a question
of look at the affect of job attributes on these processes. In doing so the
attributes applied are selective because not all aspects of work impinge
on these three processes. Within this criterion, the rationale for inclusion is
simply that they are important aspects of work that many workers share
across different sectors of tourism and across the management–worker
boundaries. More importantly these aspects have behavioural and
psychological implications. The purpose of this exercise is to highlight
meaningful differences and similarities between tourism occupations.

Aspects of Work and Their Consequences

A lot of jobs in tourism are menial yet, that pejorative label is not
always accepted by the incumbents of such roles. Without engaging the
motivational theories, to any extent it would seem reasonable to expect
that people would seek some means of satisfaction in any role. One of
the commonest views expressed by workers doing, what are ostensibly
menial jobs, is that they value something that is best summed up as *'not
factory'*. This is in fact, an example of opportunity costs oddly posing as a
'negative pleasure' – satisfaction in not doing something worse. Researchers
have been slow to explore what this motivational component actually
means but, what evidence we have, suggests it is a made up of a combination of three work attributes which are common to service jobs but
which are, in the minds of service workers, absent in factories. *These are:
(a) variety of task, which seems to embody 'dealing with people', (b) lack of
close supervision and (c) an irregular flow of work in which boredom, timing
and deadlines play a large part.* There may be more to it than this but, in
essence, it seems to imply a desire for, if not autonomy, then at least a
degree of control without a supervisor close by. It could be argued that
tolerance of low pay, discussed in the previous chapter, is a trade off for
these tacitly acknowledged benefits. This notion needs to be seen in the
context of the very imprecise labour contracts that predominate in most
forms of service work. What is 'good service' can only be subjectively
defined which means that there is an imprecision at the heart of employee
evaluation. Dealing with customers needs a degree of scope that by definition means a degree of autonomy. Supervision, whether close or distant,
has to take on board the natural autonomy in the roles. Often supervision is not physically close. In such circumstances 'standards' are set

normatively, that is, through a normative process. This requires a degree of consensus. It may well be that workers value the normative culture and bring it into their evaluation of their jobs.

An important aspect of normative behaviour within an organisation is that it is nurtured by a degree of homogeneity of knowledge across authority levels. There is always a degree of interdependence between people in an organisation based on tacit knowledge (Lam, 2000). This interdependence works vertically as well as horizontally and is the foundation of integrated work. In circumstances where managers and workers have a mutually recognised degree of shared knowledge the affect is to strengthen the assumptions that form the labour contract – thus making it more stable. In these circumstances people understand each other better. A culture of internal promotions is the recognised source of this phenomenon. It is common to tourism employment.

Putting the two arguments together, what this means is that, on the one hand, the nature of service work means a more imprecise contract but, on the other, the degree of shared knowledge makes it that much more likely that the assumptions that lie behind the contract are more mutual. The informality of labour relations described by Baldacchino (1997) is psychologically rooted in the imprecise contracts that are implicit in tourism jobs.

One incorrect assumption that is often made is that all workers, in what is classified as a service industry, are in fact service workers in any technical sense. Production jobs have finished end-products and are characterised by containing complete tasks. Many occupations within tourism actually produce things. Chefs are an obvious example. Furthermore, many tourism workers have 'complete tasks' without producing material things. Journeys would come into this category – the coach trip, the taxi ride. The significance of this type of fundamental attribute is psychological, in that, occupational psychology identifies that people have particular orientations to 'having an end product' and 'being able to work with something which is continuous'. The end product is seen as a kind of emotional home for pride in a sense of completion and satisfaction. This is often seen as the satisfaction of craftsmen. The need for an end product, to produce something material, is, in some cultures, seen as masculine work (Willis, 1979). This however, begs the question as to the basis of satisfaction when there is no end product. It is a key question in understanding service work – what is the basis of task satisfaction when tasks are continuous. One response is to socially construct an end product of which 'the satisfied customer' would be an example. Another would be the pride in coping with the challenge of variety wherein 'coping' becomes the end product. This can be destructive in some extreme circumstances (Bourdain, 2000). Often tourism jobs are concerned with the logistics of moving people where sequential dead-lines become the challenge for everyone in the chain but simultaneously such deadlines are the source of conflict. What is often *called 'technological conflict'* that is, where potential conflicts are built into the process is a conspicuous element of tourism work.

Ironically, one way of coping with constant variety, particularly for customer service workers, is to *'industrialize'* it or *'routinize'* it in the mind. In other words, bringing in the very thing that career choice led away from. What personal service work clearly displays is that variety and routine can and do co-exist in the same job at the same time. Understanding of exactly what it is that has to be coped with in service occupations had undoubtedly been enhanced by the seminal work on emotional labour by Hochschild (1983). Undertakers have to look sad, air stewards have to smile and many other service or *'boundary'* occu-pations require the manipulation of emotions that, according to Hochschild, have some adverse affects of psychological health. In many respects her position offers greater insights than the examination of stereotyping. However her position has been criticised on the grounds of exaggerating the adverse affects given the evidence of high job satis-faction in occupations where emotional manipulation applies (Wharton, 1993). The implication of this criticism is that people must be coping very well to whatever emotional adjustments jobs demand. It does however sometimes go wrong and service deteriorates. Riley (1986a, 1995), in seeking to explain those sudden downturns in aggregate levels of service which so dismay tourist destination authorities, suggests the notion of 'second position' behaviour as a coping strategy which is helpful to the employee but has adverse consequences for the customer. The idea is based on Homans' (1962) exchange theory and argues that when service encounters, for whatever reason, go wrong, workers retreat into a 'legalistic' minimal role definition. In other words, they take refuge in prescribed role definitions – 'only a job'.

Possibly more significant than surface presentation and manifest conflict is the issue of coping with inequity between the server and the served. At a higher level this issue can be embroiled in the cultural conflicts scenario that inhabits the tourism literature on hosts and guests, however, at the mundane level of daily coping emulation may seem too simplistic a solution but it has a historical track record through domestic service (Hecht, 1980). Wanting to be like the customers, identifying with them, is a form of coping with inequity and one that does not necessarily imply servility (Shamir, 1980).

Many tourism workers work unsocial hours in the sense that they are working when the general population is not. The psychological significance of this lies not so much in the hours themselves but in the fact that their hours of work isolate workers together and at the same time separate them from normal exposure to the general public. This is often compounded by geographical isolation. In other words, tourism workers often live close to each other and socialize together outside working hours. One only has to think of airports and resorts to see the geographical dimensions. What is important about isolation from the general population is the psychological process that it engenders. Basically isolation and integration mediates between the relative potency of work values and society values. The argument is not simply one of suggesting that isolation increases the significance of work. The main argument is that attitudes engendered at work are amplified by isolation. By contrast, the integration argument is that when workers go home and socialize with workers from other industries 'talking shop' is less likely and grumbles are disarmed by comparisons. In these circumstances, what happens at work stays at work.

The relevance to tourism is fairly obvious. Employees in hotels and airports are often physically isolated, working unsocial hours when the rest of the population is at leisure. In these circumstances it would be expected that work values would be fairly dominant values even out of hours, but the message for management is that this reinforcement process can work on both positive and negative raw material. The fact that the process can work in both directions puts a premium good on consistent managerial behaviour. The formation of occupational communities through isolation has important ramifications as they provide the basis for the formation of industrial norms.

It was argued earlier that the imprecision of labour contracts in service work leads to normative control and a good deal of informality. To an extent normative control may well be the appropriate form of authority but it is also impossible to ignore the effect of advancing information technology on tourism jobs (Makin *et al.*, 1996). Process engineering and standardisation practices have been applied to tourism work. There is a hidden danger here in that this strategy directly attacks the intrinsic satisfactions which workers so value. If jobs with an attractive wide scope become limited and the design of jobs becomes information-based then, employees can be managed through information. *This radically alters the nature of the psychological contract by making it more explicit and therefore more precise and from this will follow more formal labour relations.*

If the term *'service industry'* is to have any meaning it needs to distinguish itself from manufacturing industry to show what commonality

exists within it. The suggestion here is that at the heart of the difference
between service and manufacturing and the commonality within each is
the degree of precision of the psychological contract. Manufacturing jobs
tend to have end-products and outputs that can be quantified which leads
towards formal bureaucratic control. Service jobs tend be continuous and
with outputs that are difficult to quantify which leads to more informal
control. In this respect service jobs are under threat of change from
encroaching information systems and standardisation. Yet across service
industries, which must include the various sectors of tourism, workers
would recognise common attributes of work. The taxi driver and the
attraction kiosk worker would recognise the boredom of slack periods,
the hotel receptionist and the airline steward would both have to have
coping strategies for the aggressive customer, the room cleaner and the
coach driver might well bless the fact that the supervisor is distant. It is
more than just skills that are transferable – it is about identity as well.

Conclusion

The rationale for looking closely at the nature of service work was
fundamentally to highlight the commonality that exists within tourism
occupations and the differences that exist between service and production jobs. There are two implications of both differences and similarities
that are important.

First, the differences between service and production occupations
become important when issues of inter-sector labour mobility are
concerned. This aspect is explored later in the book but what can be
said at this point is that people moving from production to service have
to undergo a process of adaptation, not just at the skills level but at the
psychological level as well. To understand this it is necessary to recognise that the medium for highlighting both the similarities and the
differences is the psychological contract. It is the key to understanding
all work relationships because it is rooted in what people do and what
they are expected to do. The varying degrees of imprecision which are
caused by differential job content, imply different forms of manager-
worker relationship. It is this fact that relates the nature of work directly
to the nature of organisations.

Second, if, it is accepted that production jobs and service jobs have
different psychological contracts then managing populations of workers
with these different types of contract should be fundamentally different.
In other words there are direct implications for organisation structure.
These are the concern of organisational theory and analysis. The context

of the problem posed for organisational analysis is information technology. If more can be controlled formally, because of information technology then psychological contracts become just that much more precise. The implication of this is that it lets in more bureaucracy, particularly in the form of formality, into the management of service work. This is a hugely important issue for the future and one which is currently being addressed by organisation theory.

Part 2

Analysis: Some Empirical Studies

Chapter 6

The Principles of Biographical Analysis

Introduction

The intention in this chapter is to outline the rationale for and techniques of, the exploration of the supply side of labour. Given that in previous chapters it has been argued that the labour market is a dominant feature of the management of labour in tourism, this forms the basic rationale for placing a greater emphasis on information relating to the quality of labour supply. The basis of this information is seeking the part of the human capital of tourism workers that is accumulated through job mobility and experience. Understanding labour supply means understanding how that capital is accumulated. In other words, the assumption of this whole approach is that patterns of experience are *supply-side learning vehicles.*

Just as a recruitment officer would look at experience on a work biography the industry as a whole can capture, in aggregate terms, the levels of human capital and perhaps more importantly, how it was obtained. The emphasis on how it was obtained brings into play the issue of change and new technology. The issue here is that if, human capital is produced by patterns of experience, then changes in organisations and industrial structures will alter such patterns of experience and create new jobs and new forms of human capital. It is question of what is valuable to keep and what can be consigned to history. There is a permanent contest between the forces of stability and those of change. The argument is about the valuation of stable labour market dynamics, that is, patterns that remain constant, set against the ethos of change, which, it is suggested, contains a dangerous element of exaggeration. Biographical analysis offers the chance to look at this conundrum through empirical evidence. Such analysis attempts to integrate qualitative career analysis with new forms of labour market analysis. The behavioural assumption is that people learn by experience. Two models of learning by experience are introduced and examples of relevant techniques of measurement are described.

Why Research Qualitative Aspects of Labour Markets?

The case for looking at labour markets in this way is based on two premises, first, that the labour market is always psychologically salient to individuals. It has a background presence even for those with high job satisfaction and stable employment. Second, that the measurement of qualitative supply is, to take a simplistic line, only extending and quantifying the applied experience of organization recruiters. Recruiters assess individual biographies whereas this form of analysis does the same for aggregated data. The case for this approach to tourism labour is founded on the premise *that the labour market is a significant force in labour management within the organization.*

Labour markets are always relevant and salient to people even when they are not contemplating using it. It is part of their psychological framework that covers job satisfaction, learning and job search. It is easy to assume that individuals focus solely on the organisation in which they work and, only when job search is involved, look at other organisations. This organisation to organisation perspective is correct but the context of this exchange is the condition of the labour market. It may be that the contexts of organisation and labour market are seen as foreground and background respectively but they remain part of something whole. Where, as in tourism, the use of the labour market is for most people inescapable and a matter of custom, then this will have the effect of switching the labour market to the foreground.

In normal industrial life, information messages from the labour market arrive on the curriculum vitae of applicants. In a sense, previous experience plays a different role in selection as against recruitment. Selection handles data on an individual basis whilst recruitment makes assumptions about the availability of types of experience in the labour market. Selection is narrow whilst recruitment is broad. Yet one feeds the other. Assumptions about the labour market stem from 'impressions' gained from the throughput of individual data. The task of the aggregation of biographies is to put flesh on those impressions. To achieve this some new approaches have been developed. They build on the established field of career analysis. It follows therefore that a degree of integration is needed between career analysis and labour market analysis. The outcome of this integration is a way forward in understanding the quality of the stock of managers.

The Extension of Labour Market Analysis

Labour market intelligence is the key factor in labour market functioning that in turn is a central platform of economic development. Adam *et al.* (1992) argue that the conventional measures such as employment levels, pay statistics, quit rates, recruitment levels and educational output need to be *framed as signals* to buyers and sellers in the market. They put a high value on the publication of educational output and skills capacity. This is basically a plea for an improvement in the conventional information distribution system rather than for radically new ways of eliciting useful data. Extending the scope of labour market analysis not only enhances traditional approaches, but has value of it's own. It gives more information and different types of signals.

In a rigorous criticism of the conventional wisdom of manpower planning Psacharopoulos (1991a) pleads for greater fervour and ingenuity in labour market analysis because of the constant shortcomings in all types of forecasting. His fundamental argument is that such forecasts and extrapolations based on past and present data could be made more meaningful and accurate if the *conditions that produced the present* were better understood. Here is a distinct orientation towards the value of the past. His arguments are not a criticism of economic forecasting but a plea for useful accompanying material.

At the heart of this position is the contention that it is easy to overstate the rate of change and its impact. Such exaggeration makes it too easy to deny that much labour market activity is, in fact, stable and unchanging over time. Whilst Hage (1989) is certainly correct in stating that any change in a job produces changes in the labour market in some way, *not all changes are mould breaking!* If it is assumed that many career paths and skill accumulation patterns adapt and survive in a changing world, then this is as valuable a focus for analysis as is the much-championed changing patterns. The case is basically that, if a true portrait of the market is the objective, the stable dynamics of labour markets are as important as the changing dynamics. The consequences of ignoring stable dynamics include inaccurate forecasting, market dysfunction and the *inadvertent destruction of valuable sequences of experience, which produce the present levels of human capital.* A constant focus on change enables industry to throw the baby out with the bath water. When the effect is noticed, the cry goes up for 'more training' This is not an anti-change argument it is simply a statement that the consequences of change have implications which go deeper than a change in job content. The alternative long view would be to examine the qualitative growth factors in patterns of experience.

The Problems of Measurement: Theory and Technique

Work histories are the basic data of most approaches and draw for their theoretical foundations from the notion of biographical memory.

If work biographies are used as a form of labour market analysis, they need to be valid as a means of data collection. What is being said here is that the data collected is only as good as the accuracy with which individuals report their career histories. The use of biographical memory as a means of data collection raises certain questions. For example, how far back can people remember? What sort of bias will be found in their recollection? Can people accurately remember the specific dates that events took place? In what kind of detail can people remember past events?

There are two main ways in which work biography data can be collected. The first is the longitudinal method which would track an individual or a group of people overtime, getting them to record the detail of their working lives. The benefits of the longitudinal method are well documented and include the wealth of information that can be collected, and the accuracy of the data. However, they are also extremely time consuming, expensive and have high attrition rates. This makes the approach of using work biographies difficult for labour market analysis (Goldstein, 1979). The second approach collects work biographies using memory recall, which simply involves asking individuals to recall detailed information about their working lives. As this approach allows data collection at any point in time, for any number of given people, it is this method that is likely to be used when collecting work biographies for the purpose of labour market analysis. Given the difficulties associated with the longitudinal method, it is no surprise that collecting data by the recall/memory method is a very attractive option (Dex, 1991).

In a very fundamental way the justification for the use of biographical data rests with the discipline of Cognitive Psychology and the study of the human memory. An examination of human behaviour reveals that current activities are inescapably linked to the past. In order for a person to exist in the real world, they acquire experience of both the physical and social world. This is acquired through verbally communicated facts and direct contact with the physical environment. In addition to this general knowledge, how people view themselves (self-image) depends on placing themselves in context with what has happened in the past and what is expected to happen in the future. The process of learning from past experiences is a vital component of a person's existence. Even at a superficial level it is easy to see that coping with the present and planning for the future invariably involves drawing on past experience. The bridging of the gap between the past and the present for the individual is provided by *memory*.

The study of human memory can be approached in a number of ways. One approach is the *physical* mechanisms of the human memory, for example, biochemical changes in neural pathways, or studying the neural structures of the brain which are necessary for remembering. An alternative approach which concerns us for the collection of work biographies falls within the framework of *cognitive psychology.* This is based on the assumption that private subjective experiences of the individual combined with observed patterns of behaviour, depend on un-observable mental events involving mental processes and mechanisms. A fundamental aim of cognitive psychology is to identify these events and to determine the relationships which form this interaction. Specifically, cognitive psychology demands attention to the internal representations of past experiences and their utilisation of mental activities. A broad framework within which the study of memory may be undertaken is provided by the emphasises on the interdependence of memory and other mental processes in the discipline of cognitive psychology (Gregg, 1986). There is a vast amount of research into human memory within the cognitive psychology discipline, however, the focus here lies specifically with *autobiographical memory.*

Autobiographical Memory

Autobiographical memory is the memory for biographical information (Robinson, 1992). There are a number of definitions of autobiographical memory, for example, distinctions between memory for personal experience, and memory for general world knowledge. The first type is termed *episodic memory* which consists of personal experiences, specific objects, and people and events that have been experienced in a particular time and place. The second type, *semantic memory* consists of general knowledge and facts about the world (Tulving, 1972 cited in Cohen, 1989). This distinction has been extended to autobiographical memory where memories of personal experiences are classed as *episodic* Robinson (1976) provides a more precise definition of autobiographical memory, in this view autobiographical memory refers only to the recall of events in which a person has directly participated, as opposed to incidents in other peoples lives known only through observation or instruction. It is this part of the memory that provides the data for work biographies.

Autobiographical Memory as a Research Methodology

To understand the rationale for using work biographies in labour market analysis, it is essential to draw from a range of studies in order to collect evidence and support for the method.

Supporting evidence for the recall method will be explained with respect to six main issues: memory processes and recall; differences in memory across the lifespan; differences between reported and experienced events; the concept of self-referencing; the processes of the accuracy of event dating; and the uses of retrospective data. Each of these represents substantial justification for the validity of the research technique.

Memory recall and memory processes

An examination of research into memory recall and memory processes reveals that the way in which the human memory works facilitates a natural process whereby individuals will be able to recall past events. Reiser *et al.* (1986) examine memory search processes and retrieval strategies. They argue that autobiographical retrieval is a directed search process where retrieval strategies are employed to direct and narrow the scope of the search, in effect considering experiences likely to be relevant. Activity-based strategies, goal-based strategies, people-based strategies and time strategies are identified as classifications of information represented in knowledge structures which direct search for an experience.

Considering the retrieval process in autobiographical memories, Reiser *et al.* (1985) analyse the role of knowledge structures in the organisation and retrieval of autobiographical memories. Their research postulates the sequence of actions performed to achieve a *goal* (termed activities) are the most important influences in retrieving autobiographical experiences.

As work biographies are essentially examining careers, and as careers are goal based, and fit into any of the four identified knowledge structures (activity, goal, people and time-based), it is reasonable to assume that aspects relating to the career can be effectively remembered and recalled.

Norman and Bobrow (1979) investigate a possible viewpoint for understanding memory processes, with specific regard to memory retrieval. In considering the problems of memory retrieval, the idea is presented that the specification of what we are trying to retrieve from our memory will either be *vague* or *precise*. For memory retrieval purposes, two aspects seem to determine the level of specification that is required. First, why the information is needed and second, the alternatives that might arise were the specification incomplete. The authors call the specification of an entity a *description* and they propose that a description provides the initial specification of the records that are sought form memory. In turn, this guides the retrieval process and helps determine the suitability of retrieved records for the purpose of retrieval. The continued suggestion is that memory retrieval depends on the formation of a description of the information sought, and the failure or success of a retrieval attempt depends upon the ability to encode information at the time of storage in such a way that an appropriate description can be constructed at the time retrieval is desired. Two important aspects of descriptions are their *discriminability* and their *constructability:* how well they discriminate among all possible memory records, and how well they can be constructed at the time retrieval is required. Norman and Bobrow's claim (1979) that memory retrieval is aided by how precise the description of the memory to be retrieved is (constructability) and how easy it is to discriminate among all possible memory records (discriminability) supports work-biography research. This is because information is sought on *specific job events, therefore the descriptions of what is to be remembered have a high discriminability and are precise, therefore easier to construct.*

A further research question relates to the best way to collect memories in terms of ordering the retrieval process. Some clues are provided in research by Cohen *et al.* (1993) who provide some useful information with regard to accessing remote memories. Various studies have addressed the recall problems associated with remote autobiographical memories. Whitten and Leonard (1981 cited in Cohen *et al.*, 1993) in their research on university students asked them to recall the names of one school teacher for each year. They found the backward-ordered search was more effective than the forward-ordered or random search, put another way, it was easier to work backwards in time than to start with the first years at school and work forwards. These results imply that episodic memories are not accessed independently. In backward searching the starting point is the most recent, and therefore the most easily recalled. Once this is accessed, it aids recall to the next-to-last item which shares the same context, etc. Cohen *et al.* (1993). This is supported by Linton (1986), but is contradictory to research by Howes and Katz (1992). Howes and Katz state that subjects can recall events easier if they are asked about the most remote time period first, as the subjects 'wear out' by the time they get to the remote period. This difference can possibly be explained by the differences in the type of events to the recalled. In the study by Cohen *et al.* (1993) subjects are recalling *ordered* or *related* events, whereas Howes and Katz (1992) are asking subjects to recall *random* events.

Cohen *et al.* (1993) identify the most important features of these recall attempts. First, due to the interconnectedness of memories: one item retrieved leads on to another, therefore it is easier to work backwards from the present than forwards from a point in the past. Second, subjects were able to extend their recall far beyond the limits which appeared in initial sessions, so persistent searching does unearth memories that initially seem inaccessible. Third, retrieval of items from episodic memory depends heavily on recreating the context in which the items were orig- inally placed. Norman and Bobrow (1979) have developed a model of retrieval which fits well with these findings. They identify three stages in the retrieval process; the formation of the initial specification which consists of the description of the target to be remembered and the context, matching a retrieved item against the specification, and finally, the eval- uation which involves judging whether the retrieved item fits the initial specification. For Norman and Bobrow (1979) whether the item can be retrieved is a function of the ability to form an appropriate target descrip- tion (constructability) and the ability of that description to discriminate among all possible memories (discriminability).

The significance for the collection of work biographies is that due to the interconnectedness of memories, one item retrieved leads on to another, this suggests that the career events are linked to *time and chrono- logically ordered*. Therefore, once the respondent is thinking about their work histories the memory recall is structured which would aid the retrieval process. In addition, research suggests it is easier to work back- wards from the present than forwards from a point in the past. *The clue for work biography here is to ask individuals to recall the most recent job first, and working backwards in time. This logical sequence of jobs and career events would be helpful to memory recall.*

Differences in memory across the lifespan

As part of the justification for the recall method, one must attempt to address how far back individuals will be able to recall memories from their past. Autobiographical memory is a topic that inherently involves a lifespan approach (Rubin *et al.*, 1986). This raises questions with regard to the accuracy of memory over specified time periods. In an examination of autobiographical memories across the lifespan, Rubin *et al.* (1986) analyse the results of their own study and re-analyse three others which address this issue. The three studies examined are: Franklin and Holding (1977), Fitzgerald and Lawrence (1984) and Zola-Morgan *et al.* (1983). The comparison revealed the important finding that the data displayed the same basic pattern, which is that memories decline over the age of 40, with the increase in memories occurring at the time when the subjects were approximately 10–30 years old. Reminiscence was not present in subjects younger than the age of 30, but reminiscence is evident by the age of 50 and pronounced by the age of 60–70. All of the studies revealed that reminiscence consists of memories from when the subjects were about 10–30 years old, rather than from a given retention interval, such as four years ago (Rubin *et al.*, 1986). A study by McCormack (1979) yielded quite different results, as here the reminiscence effect is much larger. Similar findings were reported in Howes and Katz (1992) who report that more recent autobiographical memories were stronger or more accessible than very old memories. In contrast, McCormack (1979) found that the frequency of remembered events was highest for the first life quarter, with a decrease in the second and third quarter, and finally an improvement in the fourth quarter. Rubin *et al.* (1986) proposed a model to adequately describe the distribution of autobiographical memories across the lifespan. Three components are identified; a retention component for the last 20 to 30 years, which accounts for the decrease in autobiographical memories that all subjects exhibit for the most recent 20 years of their lives; a childhood amnesia for the very early years; and, a reminiscence component focusing on youth. In conclusion, the distribution of autobiographical memories across the lifespan is orderly across laboratories and across change in experimental conditions (Rubin *et al.*, 1986). Therefore, some confidence can be attributed to the conclusion that differences are evident in the memory of autobiographical events across the lifespan.

The issue of differences in *memory recall across the lifespan* has little impact on using memory recall as a research technique. Although differences in recall are evident across the lifespan, the significance is not great enough to warrant caution with regard to remembering career data. In fact, the ages of 10–30 years are postulated to be the period where memory recall is easiest. This age range covers potentially up to around 15 years of a person's career. The effects can therefore be deduced as minimal.

Differences between reported and experienced events

One of the major divisions in the research on autobiographical memory lies between the *reported* events and *experienced* events. People learn about real events in the world in two different ways; either personal experience (*directly, firsthand*) or by the report of someone else (*indirectly, secondhand*) Larsen (1988).

Brown (1990) examines the organisation of public events in long-term memory, and proposes a model of 'historical memory'. The model contains three levels of organisation; the news event; the public narrative; and the historical period, and the model allows public events to be associated with personal events. With regard to the memory of public events, Brown demonstrates that public events are often stored with accessible personal information. All public historical events shared by a large number of people also have a personal side. For example, when a public event is learned or discussed, the person is also engaged in a personal activity which can be treated as distinct events and stored as unique autobiographical memories (Brown, 1990). *In other words, contextual links form bridges between reported events and the personal context in which they were acquired.*

Using the lifespan approach, Howes and Katz (1992) examine remote memory recall for autobiographical and public events. These events from across the lifespan were examined in a sample of middle-aged (40–55 years) and older-aged adults (65–75 years). This study provides some interesting findings with regard to the ability of adults to recall both public and autobiographical events from across the lifespan:

- First, subjects tend to recall more autobiographical than public events, and in general, more events from recent than more remote periods of one's life.
- Second, more autobiographical events were recalled from the earlier periods of the subjects' lives (0–30 years), a similar number of autobiographical and public events were recalled from 31–45 years, and more public than autobiographical events were recalled for the most recent period. (46–60 years).
- Third, the older-age group recalled fewer public events than the middle-aged group across all four time periods.
- Fourth, the older-aged group's recall of autobiographical events was fairly consistent across the lifespan, whereas their recall of public events tended to increase from the earlier to the most recent period.
- Fifth, the middle-aged groups didn't have the same consistency with regard to the recall of autobiographical events. In this case, they

recalled significantly more autobiographical events for the 16–45 time span.

The study provides information on a range of findings relevant to the assessment of the autobiographical memory methodology. These are; first, *verification.* The study addresses the problems of verification for studies of memory. In the case of remembering public events, archives were consulted in order to verify what was recalled. This becomes a little more difficult with the autobiographical events. In this instance the autobiographical events were verified with the subject's spouse or close relative. The limitation must be recognised that both parties could have the same memory failure. However, despite this limitation, the authors suggest that recall from remote memory need not be subject to harsh criticism. The events appear to be recalled with accuracy. Second, *demographic variables.* The results indicate that the recall of some real-life events from remote memory is related to selected demographic variables. Recall of autobiographical information generally appears to be less susceptible to such influence. Larsen (1988) distinguished between two forms of personal memory; directly experienced events and reported events. These correspond with the current study's separation here of public (reported) and autobiographical (experienced) events. Larsen observes that few studies have been undertaken in this area, but the indirect evidence agrees and points towards the conclusion that reported public or historical events are recalled more poorly. Third, the *effect of cue words.* The task here was to discover whether cue words would disrupt the search patterns normally used by the individual and inhibit recall, or whether they would lead to more information that otherwise would have been overlooked. The evidence indicates that the former process operates in the recall of autobiographical information. Fourth, *chronological age.* In the assessment of memory for public events, it was found that the elderly perform more poorly than the middle-aged. However, this was not the case for autobiographical events where the older-age groups memory was found to be the same as the middle-aged group. The findings here support Larsen's (1988) distinction between reported and experienced events. This study also offers some explanation for the increase in autobiographical tasks reported for the 16–45 time span. A speculation is that this may be related to the frequency and importance of life events which generally occur during early and middle adulthood. Also, this evidence may support the finding that the middle-aged group reported a higher number of self-referent events than older-aged subjects. Past research reveals that self-referencing facilitates memory performance. This is indicated at least in the experimental contexts by Rogers *et al.* (1977). This increase in recall is predicted by the reminiscence period of the model put forward by Rubin *et al.* (1986). Fifth, the *time period* The conclusion here is that recall is greater for events that occurred more recently and poorer for the remote events holds only for the recall of public events Sixth, the *comparison of memory for public and autobiographical events.* For the older group, more autobiographical events were recalled than public events on both the spontaneous and the cued tasks. Furthermore, the study reveals that older people recalled significantly more pleasant events on the autobiographical tasks over the public events, which my be a significant factor.

Research by Howz and Katz (1992) concludes that autobiographical-event recall is generally superior to public-event recall, autobiographical-event recall is fairly consistent across the lifespan, and public-event recall is poorer for more distant events. This is consistent with the findings of Larsen (1988).

In support of using autobiographical recall data as a methodology, the central issue here is that autobiographical events are easier to remember than public or reported events. The superiority of autobiographical recall to reported events is a significant assurance in the recollection of personal work histories.

Importance of events relating to self

Related to the differences between reported and experienced events, the personal quality of memories (this is *my* experience) is one of the most basic phenomenal features of recall. (Robinson and Swanson, 1990). As a consequence, one of the main areas of research into autobiographical memory looks at the issue of memory events linked to the *self*. Several studies have indicated that memory for events can be improved by encoding these events in reference to the self. For example, Rogers *et al.* (1977) and Craik and Tulving (1975). Studies also examine the concept of the self-schema, which is defined as cognitive generalisations about the self, derived from past experience, that organise and guide the processing of the self-related information contained in the individual's social experience (Markus, 1977). What is important here is that the self-schema makes the individual selective about what they learn, and they are likely to remember and code things that are important to the self-schema. Brown *et al.* (1986) state the self-reference effect is explained as the familiarity of one's own self typically yields the highest memorability. Put another way, because people have more knowledge about themselves than they have about others, events encoded with respect to the self can be made more elaborate than events encoded with a different type of schema. The authors link self-reference to episodic memory and display that self-reference is part of the existing principles of memory operations, and is not a distinct mnemonic property in itself. These findings are consistent with Keenan and Baillet (1980).

Rogers *et al.* (1977) examine self-reference and the encoding of personal information. Their study is concerned with the construct of self and how it is implicated in the organisation of the person's world, as one of the main functions of the self is to help the individual process personal data. Subjects were asked to rate adjectives of four tasks designed to force the following types of encoding; structural; phonemic, semantic and self-reference. The results of the study indicate that adjectives rated under the self-reference task were recalled the best, and the authors conclude that self-reference is a powerful encoding process.

In terms of relevance to memory recall, the concept of the self-schema is important (Rogers *et al.*, 1977; Markus, 1977; Brown *et al.*, 1986). Memories which are linked to the self are more likely to be remembered and easier to recall. The self schema is cognitive generalisations about the self, derived from past experience that organise and guide the processing of the self-related information contained in the individuals self experience (Markus, 1977). *The relevance here is that individuals remember what is important to them. As a career is likely to be considered important, the details related to work will be remembered.* This is supported by Gittens (1979) who examines the reliability and recollections that can be achieved using the oral history technique. Gittens identifies that one of the most serious problems of using the oral history technique is that recollections from respondents vary over time. A solution to this is to ask specific questions, rather than general questions. It is easier for individuals to recall events they perceive as important. Also, support for the importance of the self-schema in memory recall is that memories for public or reported events can be improved by encoding these events in relation to the self (Craik & Tulving, 1975).

Linked to the idea of the self-schema, Skowronski *et al.* (1991) reviewed that psychologists have a long-standing interest in the effects of event pleasantness on memory recall. Matlin and Stang (1978) note this bias which appears in both naturalistic studies of autobiographical memories and also laboratory studies. Skowronski *et al.* (1991) indicate that event pleasantness has a significant impact on event recall, when applied to the self. When applied to others a person's a-typical event had a significant impact on memory recall. Although this suggestion is not conclusive, it can be argued that people are more likely to remember events that were either positive or negative to themselves, rather than neutral. *A job change is rarely neutral, which heightens the memorability of work related changes or events.*

Related to event pleasantness, *event memorability* has also been identified as important for remembering. Thompson (1982) measures the memory for naturally occurring episodic events, and memory for the date of occurrence of those events. Participants were asked to record a diary of unique personal events for themselves and for their roommates, and they were asked to rate the memorability of the events at the time they were recorded. This was undertaken to ascertain whether recording events improves memory for those events, and to determine whether the rate of forgetting differs for memorable and unmemorable events. The study illuminates that events rated as memorable were encoded better than events rated as unmemorable, but were forgotten at the same rate. Also, the recorder could more accurately assess the memorability of personal events than the memorability of events recorded for a roommate. In a later study, Thompson (1985) examines the implication of the self-schema in the memory for unique personal events. Using data from the previous study, Thompson illustrates the dependence of memory on the self schema. The general view that the self schema plays an important role in memory is not new. A comprehensive discussion of historical and current theorising is provided by Greenwald (1981). Thompson gives three conclusions to the implications of the self-schema. First, encoding an event with the self-schema facilitates memory more than well known techniques used to facilitate memory, for example, memory cueing. Second, familiarity with one's own knowledge structure allows one to predict one's own recall better than the recall of another individual. Third, the self-schema surpasses any other schema in the amount of information integrated in it.

In support of the recall method is the idea that event pleasantness and event memorability are linked to memory recall (Matlin & Stang, 1978; Thompson, 1982). Matlin and Stang (1978) suggest that when event pleasantness is linked to the self, people are more likely to remember events that were either positive or negative. *As a career or job change is rarely neutral, the memorability of a career event is high.*

Finally, affective memories related to *goals* is a subject which has been researched by a number of authors (see for example, Roseman (1984), Weiner (1982, 1985) and Weiner *et al.* (1979)). Affective responses to autobiographical memories and their relationships to long-term goals are examined by Singer (1990). In this research, an attempt was made to determine whether there is a connection between one's affective response to a memory, and the motivational consideration of a long-term goal.

Singer suggests that a relationship exists between an individual's affective response to a memory and the relevance of that memory to the attainment or non-attainment of specific long-term goals for an individual. *In terms of a career, job changes, promotions and personal strategies used to advance a person's career can be directly related to the attainment of career goals. It seems reasonable to conclude that memory of career-related goals would facilitate the research of work and career-related events.*

Event dating

A further issue in the collection of work biographies is to discover when specific jobs or activities took place, in other words, to obtain the date of the event. There has been considerable interest in the accuracy with which subjects can date the events they recollect which relates to the interpreting the data which respondents produce on retrospective surveys (Baddeley, 1990).

Various researchers have examined the concept of event dating within autobiographical memory research, and a number of important observations have been identified. In a series of extensive studies by Wyer and his associates (Fuhrman & Wyer, 1988; Wyer *et al.*, 1985) information has been obtained with regard to how temporal information is coded in the personal memory, and how that information is used to make temporal judgements. Fuhrman and Wyer (1988) identify that individuals appear to organise the events they are asked to recall into categories defined by the periods of life in which they occur, and assign temporal codes to these categories. Huttenlocker *et al.* (1988) examine hierarchical organisation in temporal memory, and develop a quantitative model to account for bias in event dating. Evidence is presented to support the notion that the bias evident in event dating is not necessarily due to a bias in remembering. Thompson *et al.* (1988) examine the strategies which people use when they are asked to date an event in their lives by the use of a diary study and an event generation study. In both studies, respondents used the specific reference strategy to date events, reported that when asked to reconstruct the date of an event by referencing it to another event, the other event is usually an experienced rather than a reported event. The study concludes that the specific reference strategy provides accurate dating. Huttenlocher *et al.* (1990) examine the way temporal information is represented in memory and the process used in estimating when the event occurred.

A number of authors have indicated that because the date of an event is only occasionally stored with the event, subjects must often reconstruct the date on which the event occurred (Brown, 1990; Thompson *et al.*, 1988). Research by Thompson (1985) and Thompson *et al.* (1988) indicates that the more detailed the memory for the event, the more accurate the date. Rubin (1982, cited in Cohen, 1989) checked a sample of events that subjects had recalled and dated against there own diary records, and found that 74% were correct to within one month. In a study of autobiographical memory recall Skowronski *et al.* (1991) examined the recall of self events and other events in everyday life. The results of the data indicate that event memory is only one contribution to the accuracy of event dating. Gender, person typicality and pleasantness effects were identified as significant factors. As well as this, it was revealed that event tagging also contributed to the increased date accuracy, and that self-events are more frequently tagged that other-events. *This has implications for collecting work biographies, in terms of the accuracy of remembering when job-related events, such as job changes took place. The evidence here suggests that the accuracy would be high, as we are asking individuals to recall events which are self-events which they would possibly have tagged with other events in their lives. As we are also only asking for very general dates, which we could confidently assume were correct.*

It can be argued that event dating would be accurate from a sample when asking individuals to remember when a job event took place. Jobs are self-events which possibly would have been tagged by other events in the respondents' lives. Put another way, if the clarity of event recall is an important contributor to the accuracy of dating judgements, the more a person can remember about an event, the better the date estimate will be.

Retrospective data

Given the above information, in the final section of autobiographical memory as a research methodology, the intention is to illustrate support for the retrospective method of data collection.

The quality of retrospective data is assessed using longitudinal surveys by Cherry and Rodgers (1979). The authors illustrate that opportunities arise for testing the quality of retrospective data when it is possible to link external records to self-report data on an individual basis. Studies by Douglas and Blomfield, (1956) and Yarrow *et al.* (1970, cited in Cherry & Rodgers, 1979) successfully achieved this. In this research, the authors use data from five studies to assess the quality of retrospective data. Two main limitations are identified. First, that subjects have a tendency to *over-estimate* their ability when asked to remember data with regard to skills. Second, that there is a bias in reporting for factual data and attitude data. In conclusion, a high rate of contradictory reporting and retrospective distortion of events are reported. However, despite this limitations, a number of positive conclusions are posited. The authors restate that the best a retrospective inquiry can hope to achieve is the approximation of the event or the condition experienced by the subject. Also, bias is likely to be reduced if there is some understanding of intervening events and their possible effect on the later report. Put another way, retrospective inaccuracy is not solely a function of time, but includes the experiences and opinions which have happened to an individual over time. For example, people who leave an apprenticeship without completing it are likely to change their job completely. As a result, a person currently in police work would seem less likely to recall a period in apprenticeship training than the person on the next bench who is now a skilled fitter (Cherry & Rodgers, 1979). The authors conclude that the above assessment is not encouraging for those involved in ad hoc retrospective enquiries, and at the planning stage it is essential for the researcher to determine the relative importance and severity of possible data biases and inaccuracies.

Peters (1989) offers a direct comparison of Panel Data versus Retrospective data in the analysis of lifecycle events, with specific focus on marital history. It is noted that until the mid-1960's studies for the US population of lifecycle events were based on cross-sectional data sources or on retrospective surveys. The problems of cross-sectional data are well documented (Hobcraft *et al.*, 1982, cited in Peters, 1989), and whilst retrospective data addresses some of these issues, they are often biases because of inaccurate recall of events or of dates of events. Panel data alleviates the limitations of both of these methods as they contain lifecycle events by gathering information at a specific point closer to the event, enabling easier recall. However, due to the enormous costs involved in panel surveys, an importance is placed upon assessing the quality of information with regard to lifecycle events that can be obtained from one shot retrospective surveys (Peters, 1989). The study reveals the important conclusion that when a marital event is reported from both sources there is substantial agreement about the date of the events. In addition, the sources do equally well in estimating hazard rate models of first marriage, divorce and remarriage. When errors do occur, the errors appear to relate to factors which increase the difficulty of recall in retrospective histories.

The limitations of human memory in respect of the design for retrospective surveys is addressed by Baddeley (1979). The study commences with an investigation of the determinants of forgetting, and proceeds with a look at possible bias and distortion in what is remembered. The forgetting curve, retroactive interference, proactive interference are examined with regard to the determinants of forgetting, and memory distortions are explained by prior expectations, leading questions, and emotive conclusions. The implications of these aspects of human memory in the design of retrospective surveys are that the most obvious conclusion from human memory psychology is that forgetting will occur and this would place constraints on the interpretation of results. The accuracy can be improved if subjects are asked about the last occurrence of any given event, only asking for details of one out of many similar events as the various incidents will confuse each other, and the time between the event and the survey should be minimised since forgetting and distortion increases over time. Finally, as people tend to remember in terms of previous assumptions and beliefs, leading questions should be avoided.

Moss (1979) provides an overview of the recall method in social surveys. The overview states with confidence that the use of retrospective data – asking informants to recollect experiences or behaviour – will remain a necessary research tool. Three main reasons are cited for this. First, economic, as the research is much cheaper than longitudinal surveys, second, the shortcomings of the research method are not necessarily final, and third, new research can build on and improve existing work.

It would appear to be important to recognise the difficulties and bias which apply to retrospective data. However, the technique is a useful one that has successfully been applied to many surveys, the merits of which would translate into studies of work biography.

Summary of the recall method

The aim of this section has been to provide support for using autobiographical memory and the recall method in order to obtain detailed work biographies. The following points are gathered as evidence:

- autobiographical events are successfully remembered from across the lifespan, and the recall of autobiographical events is superior to the recall of public events;
- the recall of autobiographical events improves if events are important to the self-schema, linked to long term goals, event memorability and event pleasantness;
- a directed and focused recall of events beginning with the most recent event first and working backwards in time improves the memory recall process;

- the accuracy of the description of the event to be recalled improves the memory recall process;
- the accuracy of event dating improves if the events are important to the self-schema, and the description of the event is detailed; and
- retrospective biographical data can confidently be assumed to be a successful research methodology.

Research Design Techniques

There are two working models that can be applied to research on experience, these are; first, the additive model in which skills and knowledge are accumulated brick by brick, and second, the development model which is concerned with the change in ability produced by a change of job. In the first model research looks at the jobs in the career sequence whilst in the second the focus is on the difference between those jobs. In terms of research the additive model presents fewer problems. The techniques of qualitative supply measurement are, for the most part, based on the additive model. Research on developmental models is progressing.

Work histories are always a sequence of jobs. If these work histories have the character of elevation we normally call them careers but whatever they are called the basic vehicle of analysis is the sequence. The interpretation of sequences involves answering key questions such as, is there a logic behind the sequence? Is there an accumulation of skill and knowledge? How coherent is the resulting human capital? How relevant to what is needed today is that human capital? Is there a key stage in the sequence that has a determining effect on the rest of the sequence? If there is elevation, in the sense of a career, what was the rate of climb? Are there any antecedents of a change in the rate of climb?

On the assumption that no sequence can be analysed unless its direction is known, it follows that the first question to ask is, 'is there a direction or is it just drifting around?'. It becomes easier to answer this question if the sample is taken from one target job or a cluster of related jobs. One of the new approaches to labour markets does in fact cut cross-sections out of the labour market for examination this is more complicated than the job targeting approach (Burchell, 1992). Targeting not only gives the analysis some direction but also allows for comparisons. However, by far the most important problem is the classification of experience. The overall design issues can be stated as:

(a) designing a sample – built around a target job;
(b) finding a meaningful classification of the experiences;

(c) locating the direction and elevation of the sequences;
(d) locating important stages in a sequence; and
(e) combining individual data into an aggregate format.

What is to be measured when we measure experience? The problem of developing a classification system to cope with this shares the generic problem of occupational classification schemes in that they have to ask 'what do people do?' and job labels are not too helpful. It is however, not quite the same problem because a sequence of job changes between organisations means that the comparative job 'level' becomes not just an element of job activity, as in a normal classification problem but the most crucial arbiter of the success of the classification. Chapter 10 illustrates the problems of developing normal occupational classification schemes applied to tourism.

There are numerous options in job classification, such as, classify by level of knowledge, type of knowledge, status, function, specific activity, and the form of change between old job and new job. In pragmatic terms the basic choices come down to describing by function or by skills or by knowledge. They can all be incorporated into the concept of experience. Functions can be added and skills and knowledge can be captured through techniques related to the development model. However, there is a sense in which these descriptions are low common denominators. What they have difficulty capturing are the larger abilities such as, the skill to synthesize fragmented data into a coherent picture, vision, political strategy, and self assessment-all aspects that might be important to certain types of job of which management would be a clear example. Notwithstanding these issues, the problems of measuring the hierarchical level of dimension has to be addressed in sequence tracing across markets.

Some relevant techniques

If the problem is to analyse career paths, then the key issues are capturing mobility in the labour market and identifying key and salient stages. Some of these issues are resolved by a measurement technique. This is the case with identifying particularly salient stages and displaying paths. One technique, which is based on target job sampling, not only offers a way of tracing paths but also of highlighting salient stages. Known as the biographical age distribution it works from a target occupation (Riley, 1993a).

This techniques was developed from conventional age distributions and based on the principles of the 'camel model'. Within large organisations age distributions are used as manpower planning and pension-planning

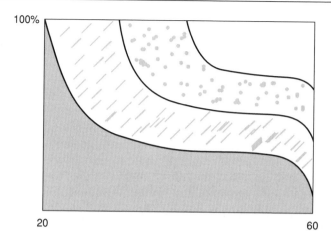

Figure 6.1 Conventional age distribution

tools. An age distribution is basically a photograph of an organisation at a particular point in time. It displays *the proportion of employees in a particular grade at each age.* Figure 6.1 is an example of an organisation with four levels. The X axis is a range of ages from 20 to 60 and the Y axis is the percentage of employees in each of the four grades.

Such a distribution can meet several needs of career analysis. For example, it can identify stages of progression by locating the probable age limit when people move up a grade. Indicating the last age before the graph line between each grade begins to go horizontal does this. It can identify streams given the assumption that those that go up first go further and it can identify previous surges and blockages in the promotion system (Keeney *et al.*, 1980). The turn-down at the end of each line suggests the propensity to upgrade employees just before their retirement. For an illustration of these attributes see Bennison and Casson (1984).

Figure 6.2 is a different type of age distribution known as the biographical age distribution. Its task is identical with the conventional type only it is conceived to handle career sequences between organisations. Here the conditions are changed from describing different people of different ages in different grades as in the organisational type, to describing *the same people at different ages in different grades.* In other words, the distribution now looks backwards over the biographical histories of a sample taken from the market not one organisation. The basic requirement for such a distribution is a target occupation that functions as a directional

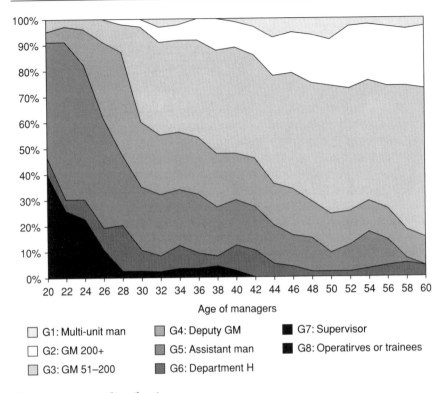

Figure 6.2 Age distribution

anchor. In other words the sample have all reached the target job and the interest is in tracing back their journey.

Figure 6.2 is based on management jobs and displays the progress of a population through eight levels of management to a particular managerial position (Riley, 1995a). All the sample subjects currently hold the target job (G2) and the research is looking backwards over careers expressed in proportions. Notice how little G7 and G6 contribute to the career path.

This distribution contributes to the important question of what constitutes a salient stage. If a salient stage can be defined as one in which a large proportion of the sample who have reached the target job spent the largest amount of time, then this stage can be said to be salient. It is admittedly a very rough definition. In this example G3 and G4 appear to be salient and require elaboration. The application of the biographical age distribution is illustrated in Chapter 8.

The problem of variation and classification

The biographical age distribution is applicable when there is a clear target job and, more importantly a sequence towards that target which can be successfully classified. This may not always be the case. Instead the following condition might pertain in relation to an area of job study:

- There is considerable role differentiation between organisations.
- There are possibly numerous technical functions associated with the job.
- There is variation in level of authority between organisations.
- There is a wide range of salaries associated with the job title.
- There is no standardised corpus of knowledge associated with the job.
- There is no formal qualification or professional qualification.

Given that job title and level of authority are essential items the question for the researcher is to say what data will collected from the biographies under those headings. Depending on the model being used, details of work histories can be extended to the limits of a questionnaire. In the additive model job titles and authority levels form the basic data that is then filled out by whatever work classification scheme is being used. In this way every job has a title, a level of authority and is described in a predetermined way. This data is augmented by contextual information such as the size of the organisation and the locus of control. Obviously the degree of detail governs the depth of the analysis but this should be determined at the outset of the research. The key issues here are, how much information is conveyed by job titles and levels and what should be the basis of the classification scheme. This last aspect is like saying' what is to be added up?'. Whatever the design the objective is always the same to give sufficient description to answer the main questions on the patterns found. The need for, and problems of, job classification schemes in circumstances of high job content variation is explored by the studies in Chapter 10.

Perhaps the simplest of the additive methods is the template approach that is particularly suitable for occupation where the skills can easily be identified. This method involves using a team of experts to specify what skills and knowledge are required by a target job and to differentiate it by levels. The expert's judgements must possess a degree of concordance in both content and level. Given that job title and level of authority are essential items, the question for the researcher is to say what data can be collected from the biographies under those headings. Depending on the model being used, details of work histories can be extended to add organisational data subject to the limits of a questionnaire.

The Increasing Need to Embrace Qualitative Labour Market Analysis

The discussion so far has centred upon the general case for improving qualitative supply information and on showing that, in the case of managerial labour supply, it is possible to generate useful data. There are, however, more specific reasons behind both ideas. Although it has been argued that stable dynamics are as valuable as changing dynamics and that the greater value placed on change can lead to market dysfunction. Unknowingly vital experience sequences can be cut. However, there is a certain irony in the fact that the main case for increasing interest in labour market analysis comes from new patterns of organisational change.

Much of the radical change is conspicuous – the breakdown of functions, standardisation, flatter hierarchies, increasing work flexibility and the informal integration of firms across competitive boundaries (Marin & Mayntz, 1991; Storper & Scott, 1990). Work biographies are going to look very different in the face of these changes. One outcome may be a greater level of inter-firm mobility. By strange irony, flatter organisations increase the possibility of upward mobility because of the homogeneity of knowledge they encourage but simultaneously reduce the actual opportunity because of the reduced numbers at higher levels (Ghiselli, 1969). The increasing standardisation implies a lowering of job scope which automatically changes the nature of experience and places limitations on the organisation's capacity to develop the individual. Both these trends will impel individuals towards the labour market in career planning.

The thrust of the argument here is that a greater understanding of how the present came about is valuable market information. This understanding comes from qualitative measurement. One technique has been illustrated to show that such measurement is possible. It must be said that measurement of this kind is new and researchers are still exploring the possibilities. By far the hardest problem is finding a classification scheme that is both meaningful and feasible.

In a very real sense the true beneficiary of this type of research is training. What it will do is to put a stop the exaggeration of the potency of training and let it live in a more realistic environment. The movement towards 'freeing up' the labour market by advocating the primacy of skill over that of occupation is an idea in search of data. This type of analysis would assist. In many countries there are substantial difficulties involved in organising training. These efforts often go hand in hand with market dysfunction. What is required is a *balance between new thinking on change and valuing old supply lines.*

Conclusion

The principles of biographical analysis have been demonstrated as a way in which to understand the supply side vehicles of the labour market. The fundamental approach is the idea that we can learn from the past – and that an understanding of past labour market trends and how capital is accumulated gives vital indicators of the supply side of labour. Although the technique is in its infancy, and is not without some problems, biographical analysis is an effective mechanism for learning about the supply side of labour in terms of experiences and the accumulation of human capital. Importantly, the technique has been demonstrated to work successfully as an exploratory tool in dynamic labour markets. This is an essential requirement for labour market analysis applied to the tourism and hospitality labour supply.

Chapter 7
Mobility into Tourism

Introduction

In much of the hospitality literature *mobility* is seen from the unit management perspective and as such is normally conceived as 'a problem'. In Chapters 3 and 4 we turned the tables on this perspective and suggested that, although it may cause operational difficulties, it is in fact a solution to the problem of controlling labour costs. It produces deflationary pressure on labour costs and acts as an aid to productivity. In Chapter 7 however, we take a wider perspective. The question that is addressed below has a broader significance. We ask, from where in the economy do the people who take up jobs in tourism come from. The obvious assumption here is that some part of the tourism workforce enters the industry from other sectors. If true, then studying inter-sector mobility is as important a part of understanding tourism employment as studying the inter-organisational mobility that so troubles management. The key process in this chapter is mobility in all its forms. Of particular interest is mobility that terminates in tourism.

Human Capital and Labour Mobility

At the heart of the notion of labour mobility is the concept of human capital – the stock of an individual's skills and knowledge. Under normal economic circumstances remuneration increases as human capital increases. In economic theory, human capital is used to explain the distribution of remuneration within a society. Within this framework, skill and pay levels would be expected to be consistent across industries with inter-sector mobility maintaining that consistency (Groshen, 1991). In other words, jobs requiring the same amount of human capital would carry similar rewards across different industries or firms. In a stable economic system, the effects of human capital would be subject to pressure from demand variables such as size, structure and rate of expansion–contraction. In any circumstances patterns of labour mobility would be expected to reflect the distribution of rewards underpinned by human capital (Becker, 1975).

The actual process by which people acquire and use their human capital is described by a number of models. According to the reward-resource model (Tuma, 1976), individuals seek to ensure that their human capital is commensurate with their job rewards. The process through which this is realised is mobility. Whilst this model assumes that individuals have unlimited opportunities to reach equilibrium between their resources and the reward from their job, the limited opportunity model suggests that there are situations and individuals who are restricted by their lack of opportunities. In this case, the lack of a better alternative induces individuals not to use mobility but to retain their current job (Hachen, 1990).

Given the fact that mobility is conditioned by human capital, the skill differentials between two industries are important especially when one is in decline whilst the other is expanding. It is plausible to suggest that expanding industries with low human capital requirements become the obvious recipient of displaced labour that is, labour shed by contracting industries (Szivas & Riley, 1999). This process will depend not only on the skill differences but also willingness to adapt and learn. These processes themselves involve motivation. In this sense, expanding industries with low skills become the destination for the 'refugees' from other industries because entrance is relatively easy. It is likely that an individual, who has been separated from his knowledge and skills, would be disorientated and would seek employment at the earliest opportunity. *Low skills industries, therefore, might offer a vehicle for such individuals to get back to the labour market.* In these circumstances, the commonly found relationship in which geographical mobility engenders occupational mobility is likely to be exaggerated (Schroeder, 1976). The literature on geographical mobility suggests that when people change location there is a tendency for them to also change career. Similarly, the tendency of organisation size diversity and job diversity within an industry promotes both inter-organisational mobility and job mobility and by so doing serves to facilitate new entries (Greve, 1994). In other words, if an industry contains a wide range of enterprises of different size and a wide range of jobs therein, then inter-industry mobility will be encouraged because there are always vacancies for new entrants to take up.

The Mobility Decision

Following the human capital argument, one way to look at the decision to change job would be as a cost benefit calculation. In the scheme the cost of moving (both in economic, social and psychological terms) is compared with the expected benefits (e.g. increased income, improved working conditions or quality of work). The aim of the individual, in this perspective, is to maximise the return on the human capital investment (Mallier & Shafto, 1989).

This is not a new idea. A useful guideline is provided by Adam Smith (1776) who pointed out the various considerations that affected the choice of a job. These were:

(1) The agreeableness or disagreeableness of the employment, the hardship involved and the honourableness or dishonourableness of the employment.
(2) The difficulty and expense of learning.
(3) The constancy and security of employment.
(4) The trust reposed in those who perform the job.
(5) The probability of success in the job.

Adam Smith was explaining the determinants of wage levels by evoking the complexity of economic, market and psychological variables that affect job choice. It was argued in Chapter 4 that pay levels and mobility had a causal relationship. Whilst it would be easy to argue that, in the case of mobility towards a higher paid sector, the pay differential was a motivating factor, the full complexity of motives is required to explain why people move into a sector with lower pay. In addition to the motivational factors there are structural considerations. Mobility is not entirely random – the labour market always has a form and structures that channel mobility.

When examining the dynamics of mobility, a question that naturally arises is to what extent does the past play a part in the mobility decision. Maillat's (1984) idea of mobility channels suggests that jobs form linkages with each other and that any job leads only to a limited number of other jobs. In this respect each job has a particular function in the career of the individual: a job can provide stability, serve as a springboard or offer flexibility. What Maillat is assuming here is that there is a degree of continuity of human capital. This may not always be the case and people jump gaps and change direction completely – with or without the aid of retraining. There are also jobs that are not tied to the labour market, and losing or giving up these jobs means an exit from the labour market. Seasonal work is one such employment.

We can argue that the pattern of inter-industry mobility is influenced by the characteristics of the person's pre-mobility industry and that the differential in human capital between that which has been acquired and that needed in a new job has both economic and psychological importance. At the heart of the argument is the recognition that the acquired skills in that industry and the value of those skills in the new industry are crucial for the economic well-being of the individual. In other words, the skills acquired previous to the mobility have a strong influence on the prospects and the direction of the job search in relation to the new industry. To an extent, this idea is problematic to the case of *'dislocation'* where the old human capital is deemed redundant. The influence of the old skills on the new is dependent on the existence of similar jobs (Fallick, 1993). As a summary, what Fallick (1993) is saying is that there needs to be a degree of accumulation in job changes and Maillat (1984) is suggesting the local labour market confirms this by employment channels between 'similar' jobs.

Factors Influencing Inter-industry Mobility

Inter-industry mobility is influenced by a number of circumstances, primary among these, as has been stressed before, is human capital. The availability of skills and the transferability of skills are the important issue here. On the one hand, people with higher education might be more able to change jobs but, on the other, it means a higher risk for them (Greve, 1994). It is not just the level of human capital that counts there is the crucial element of specificity. The more job-specific and industry-specific human capital is then the probability of job mobility declines (Becker, 1975). Industry-specific human capital reduces the propensity for inter-industry mobility. The opposite applies in the argument, where skills are generalised mobility increases. What follows from this argument is that mobility is more likely to occur in unskilled workers not because the level of human capital is low but because it is generalised and transferable. Tourism might be a good example of this.

Personal characteristics such as the labour force experience of the worker, age and gender are factors that influence the overall mobility of the individuals. Amongst these factors job tenure stands out. Often correlated with age, job mobility decreases with the extending job tenure. By contrast, there is support for the idea that a high number of previous jobs indicate higher propensity to leave the present job (Greve, 1994).

Wage levels are the mechanisms which link industrial characteristics like job concentration, labour intensity and industrial growth to job mobility (Hachen, 1992). Inter-industry differences in wage levels are thought to have a strong explanation in industrial characteristics like employment concentration and profit rates (Groshen, 1991). Slichter (1950) found that industry differentials are consistent across skill levels and vary positively with corporate income and negatively with labour intensity. In other words, mobility produces a consistent pattern of reward for skills across industrial boundaries with only company success and employment density interfering in the process.

Unemployment rate is related with inter-industry mobility and the relationship is explained by two, conflicting, theories. According to the first theory, a high rate of unemployment leads to a reduced mobility rate. This 'chilling effect' on mobility is explained both by the climate of job insecurity and by the tendency of employees to use seniority as a protection against layoff. Opposed to this theory, according to the sectoral shift theory by Lilien (1982), is the shift between industry sectors in terms of demand for labour and the consequent mismatch between skills offered by the unemployed and skills required, results in frictional and structural unemployment. This leads to higher unemployment which increases the incidence of inter-industry mobility. One theory suggests an 'ossification' of the market because of insecurity the other suggests surge in mobility as people attempt, out of necessity, to move sectors

Types of Mobility

Until now the discussion has mostly focused on inter-industry and job mobility, but there are other types of labour mobility as well that we have to consider! Some people would change industries or jobs using the same skills and knowledge as before, while others would experience an additional change, that of an occupation. An example of the first case might be an accountant who has moved from working in manufacturing industry to a job as an accountant at a tour operator. A school teacher opening a beach bar or a farmer taking up a job as a waiter would represent the second case.

When moving between jobs, occupations or industries, people often move geographically as well, hence we can see that mobility can manifest itself in a number of ways. These are:

- job mobility;
- occupational mobility;
- inter-industry mobility;
- geographical mobility.

Some Methodological Problems

The principal methodological issues have been addressed in Chapter 6. However one issue remains and that is the use of a standard classification system for identifying economic sectors. Most countries have some form of classification in official economic statistics. The diversity of the industry, outlined in Chapter 1 requires any study of tourism to make decisions about the identity of its occupations. The case study to be described on tourism employment is interpreted in its wider context comprising of the following sectors of the industry:

- hotels;
- guest houses;
- restaurants;
- cafes;
- travel agency;
- transportation; and
- other; mainly souvenir shops.

Mobility into Tourism: A Study from Hungary

Methodology and sample

The research focused on inter-industry mobility that terminated in tourism. The locale of the study was Hungary during the transition from communism to a market economy.

The primary data was collected through self-completed questionnaires. The subjects were individuals who had moved into tourism from another industry. The main thrust of the methodology was to analyse the actual patterns of mobility, explore the motives and measure the impacts related to the mobility decision. The character of the questionnaire was biographical and based on the concept of autobiographical memory (Dex 1992). The design followed the principles explored in career structure research (Ladkin & Riley, 1996; Riley, 1990;). The definition of tourism workers was pitched fairly wide and included workers in hotels, restaurants, cafes, travel agents, taxi drivers, coach drivers and shop workers in tourist centres.

Six hundred questionnaires were sent to a random sample of tourism workers in four selected areas of Hungary. The sample returned was 351, resulting in a 58.5% response rate. The sample contains 202 female (58%) and 149 male (42%) subjects. The average age was computed at 37.05 years. Given the general observation that younger people tend to

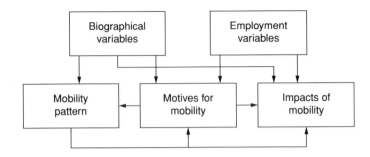

Figure 7.1 The inter-relatedness of the variables

be more mobile than older ones, it is interesting that 52.6% of the sample was over the age of 35. The majority of the respondents (62.96%) had secondary school education.

Figure 7.1 illustrates the inter-relatedness of the variables used in the study. The relationship between the variables is indicated by the direction of the arrows which are pointed from the independent variables towards the dependent variables. It has to be pointed out that the examination and discussion of motives for the mobility will be dealt with separately in Chapter 9.

Background to the study

Before commencing to present the study findings it is necessary at this point to briefly examine the prevailing economic and social conditions that set the background to the study.

Characterised by an over-emphasised industrial base and an underdeveloped service sector, structural changes were inevitable for the Hungarian economy by the end of the 1980s. Two major aspects of the structural adjustment process have implications for the study. First, it was accompanied by a serious contraction of the economy, one that can be best described by the fact that, over the four-year period from 1989 to 1993 the Gross Domestic Product (GDP) fell by 20%. Second, the structural changes were a consequence of a differential contraction of all industries rather than a net result of growth in some industries and a decline in others. While the GDP of the so called 'material branches' of the economy (manufacturing, construction and agriculture) fell by 28% during this period, that of the service sector dropped only by 5% (Pukli, 1994).

Until 1986 the Hungarian economy had been officially claimed to be working at full employment. With 6,400 unemployed, the unemployment rate started off at a negligible level in 1987 but increased rapidly between 1990 and 1993. By 1993 the unemployment peaked at 663,000 – equal to a 12% unemployment rate which fell away to settle at around 10%. Behind the national unemployment figure there is a severe regional imbalance and a high proportion of long-term unemployed (Fazekas, 1995).

In neo-classic economic theory the factors which influence job choice in market conditions are based on comparative advantage of different types of work assuming complete information. In broad terms, this perspective can be mirrored at the aggregate level by inter-sector comparisons. Accepting, of course, that the macro-level data do not represent the actual knowledge base of individual job seekers. The first task in using national statistics is to find how they display tourism employment and earnings. Unfortunately for the study, secondary information on industrial labour conditions was found to be incomplete. However, the pay data indicated a position that was so emphatic that it was usable. Table 7.1 shows the relative pay based on the official Hungarian classification. Tourism workers are distributed in a number of classes but for the purpose of analysis we have taken the category 'hotel and restaurant' as the general indicator of pay levels in tourism. The monthly net earnings are shown in Hungarian currency (Forint).

Table 7.1 clearly indicates that during a period of wage inflation, employment in tourism receives the lowest pay category. Notwithstanding the absence of other employment data which might offset the implications of Table 1, it is very clear that a move into tourism would, for most people, involve a decrease in pay. How far the official figures depart from actual earnings is not known but even a severe underestimation would still leave tourism employment close to the bottom of the earnings ladder. The unemployment picture is such that it might suggest that with other industries declining tourism might be a source of employment no matter what the pay.

Study findings

The pattern of mobility

The questionnaire asked subjects to give their employment pattern over the period of 1987–1996. They were to include periods of unemployment, deliberate absence from the labour market and periods in education. Through this data it was possible to trace the patterns of employment leading towards tourism.

Of the total sample, 80.63% (283 respondents) moved into tourism during this 10 year period. The analysis of inter-sector mobility is therefore based

Table 7.1 Monthly net earnings by industries in Hungary in
Hungarian Forint (1985–1995)

Industry	1985	1990	1991	1992	1993	1994	1995
Agriculture	5,408	8,817	10,001	11,710	14,127	18,261	21,338
Mining			16,256	18,907	23,426	28,560	31,895
Manufacturing	6,172	10,273	12,316	14,976	17,924	22,573	25,790
Energy			14,989	18,498	22,174	27,897	31,924
Construction	6,352	10,586	12,014	14,332	16,685	21,292	22,496
Trade/Repair	5,409	10,330	12,754	15,656	18,376	22,722	24,359
Hotel/Rest			11,067	13,844	16,274	20,052	20,829
Transport	6,301	9,844	13,101	16,403	19,047	24,456	27,351
Finance			20,681	26,329	31,663	38,542	41,659
Public adm			17,561	17,546	21,860	26,888	29,462
Education			13,003	15,479	17,033	22,463	24,095
Health			12,397	14,580	16,059	21,127	22,915
National average	5,929	10,108	12,889	15,628	18,397	23,424	25,891

Source: Compiled from Statistics by the Hungarian Office of Statistics

on this sample and does not include the remaining 68 respondents who
moved into tourism prior to this period.

Industry prior to moving into tourism

Given the significantly different stage of development in Hungary, the
study did not expect a dominant flow from agriculture but it was
expected to identify a fairly restricted number of industries providing
workers for tourism. Furthermore, in line with the hypothesised role of
tourism as a refuge for the victims of transition, it was anticipated that
a number of respondents would have exchanged their unemployed position with a job in the tourism industry. Figure 7.2, which is based on
the official classification of industries, shows which sector of the economy
the tourism workers came from.

Figure 7.2 illustrates a rather broader than expected source of labour
for tourism. The wide range of industries can be best illustrated by the
fact that, with the exception of mining, mobility into tourism occurred
from every sector of the economy. The highest category is trade which
provides 20.85% of the sample. According to the Hungarian terminology,
trade includes both retailing and foreign trade companies. The second
category 'other' amalgamates those coming from the service sector (e.g.

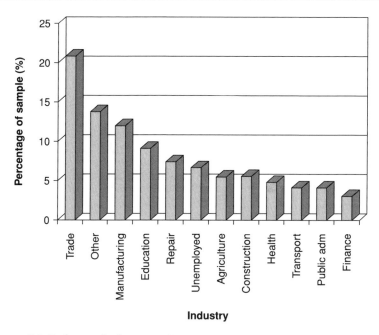

Figure 7.2 Industry before tourism

hairdressers), those having lived abroad, housewives and those on maternity leave. With 13.78% they represent a considerable portion of the sample. The third industry on the list is manufacturing where 12.01% of the sample came from. The decline in manufacturing industries with the resulting redundancies is the likely inducement of this mobility.

The conspicuous characteristic of the data lies in the fact that the list of industries nearly exhausts the whole economy. The education sector (9.19%) is the fourth sector indicating that deteriorating social status and low pay in education make tourism an attractive employment option. For the 6.71% of the sample who changed their unemployed status for employment, tourism provided a channel back to the labour market.

Apart from inter-industry mobility, the study also examined the geographical mobility and the job status mobility of the sample. From the 283 respondents who have moved into tourism since 1987, 33 (11.7%) moved geographically when taking up a tourism job or starting a tourism business. The relationship between geographical mobility and inter-industry mobility was an important measure because it was assumed that mobility from certain industries into tourism would necessitate a geographical relocation.

The self-evaluation of the impact of mobility

Having established the pattern of mobility, what follows now is the presentation of the findings on the *direction and magnitude* of change which occurred as a result of the mobility into tourism. The analysis is based upon the subjective evaluation of the impacts of the change by the respondents. The analysis includes data from the total sample and thus contains data from 351 respondents.

Ten dimensions have been evaluated by the respondents on a five-point Likert-scale ranging from: (1) Significantly improved to (5) Significantly worsened. The dimensions were:

- Job security.
- Career prospects.
- Social status.
- Physical environment.
- Standard of living.
- Control over work.
- Working hours.
- Job satisfaction.
- Compatibility between education and skills required by the job in tourism.
- Income.

The proposition which guided the analysis of change is that, given the economic transition, and that some people would enter tourism as a contingency, the level of satisfaction would be low. This is reinforced by the fact that the macro-level pay data (Table 7.1), at least as far as the hotel and restaurant sector is concerned, suggest a relative pay disadvantage to those engaged in other economic sectors. Given the fact that two thirds of the sample moved into that sub-sector, a worsening living standard and a pay decrease was anticipated for the majority of the sample. Furthermore, it was thought that in some cases subjects – either voluntarily or forcibly – would have given up jobs with higher social status in order to secure employment or to enjoy certain positive aspects of tourism employment. Given the intrinsic character of tourism jobs to involve long and unsocial working hours, the dimension of working hours was expected to be appraised as one with a negative change.

The mean values and standard deviations (SD) derived from a five-point scale for the change items are shown in Table 7.2 In order to facilitate the interpretation of the data, the direction of change as set by the mean value will be given in the fourth column. Given the coding method, a mean value of 3 would indicate a 'no change' position, while

Table 7.2 Means and standard deviations for ten dimensions ($n = 351$)

Dimension measured	Mean value	SD	Change
Job security	2.567	1.1	Positive
Career prospects	2.624	0.9	Positive
Social status	2.687	0.8	Positive
Physical environment	2.306	0.9	Positive
Standard of living	2.431	0.8	Positive
Control over work	2.366	0.7	Positive
Working hours	2.842	1.1	Positive
Job satisfaction	2.239	0.8	Positive
Education/job match	2.726	0.9	Positive
Income	2.347	0.9	Positive

higher figures represent a negative impact. Values below 3 indicate that the impact of the mobility into tourism was evaluated as positive.

The picture shown in Table 7.2 is one of general contentment which can be best illustrated by the fact that, contrary to the hypothesis, none of the dimensions were appraised to have worsened. The mean values for the remaining ten dimensions range from 2.239 for *job satisfaction* to 2.842 for *working hours*.

Despite the hypothesised relative pay disadvantage when moving into tourism, *income* (2.347) is rated as having improved! The *standard of living* (2.431) improved slightly less than income, a difference probably due to a general feeling of worsening living conditions of wage earners in Hungary.

The most positive impact of the mobility into tourism for the total sample was reported on the job satisfaction variable. With a mean value of 2.239 (SD = 0.8), for the majority of the respondents the industry change has resulted in an increased job satisfaction.

Conclusion

This chapter showed a methodology for capturing mobility flows into tourism. The data showed that – in the Hungarian context- people came from virtually every sector of the economy. This occurred in a situation when comparative earnings in tourism were below those in most industries. Despite this, the data showed high levels of contentment.

The study examined a further element of mobility which was triangulated with the above two dynamics. This third element is the motivational aspect which will be discussed in Chapter 9.

Chapter 8

Career Analysis and Labour Markets: A Study of the Career Paths of Hotel Managers

Introduction

The purpose of this chapter is to illustrate how career analysis needs to be linked to labour market dynamics in order to gain a clear picture of how careers progress in a market-led industry. The premise behind this approach is that it is impossible to understand how careers are planned and developed without considering the labour market characteristics in which they operate. As a form of investigative manpower planning, career analysis set in the labour market context is able to provide us with a detailed insight into how careers are developed and progressed in a market context. Central to this idea are career opportunities and structure. Career opportunities are not infinite, as they are determined by the size and structure of the industry or profession for which an individual is qualified for. Structural features include the size of the industry, the degree of fragmentation in the industry, the shape of the organisational pyramid, the distribution of knowledge, and technological specificity (Ladkin & Riley, 1996). Certain types of industry framework promote bureaucratic career structures, for example, large organisations with structured career routes, whilst other forms encourage a labour market-orientated approach. Where the structure is fragmented, the units small, the technology low level, and where knowledge is homogeneously distributed about the pyramid, there is a greater propensity for mobility. An analysis of hotel labour market behaviour suggests that the structure of the hotel industry is of this type, and encourages a high level of self-directed mobility for career progression (Riley, 1991). If, as the case of the hotel industry illustrates, it is the market as an entity in itself, as distinct from organisations, that leads career progression.

The sequence of arguments begins with an outline of the key concepts of career analysis and labour market dynamics, and then proceeds to explore how these two are linked. In order to illustrate how career analysis needs to be studied in the context of labour market dynamics the example of the careers of hotel managers is used.

Career Analysis

To understand career patterns and processes, a detailed investigation of individuals' careers is required. The research technique used for achieving this detailed investigation is called career analysis. Career analysis is a form of work history analysis, and is concerned specifically with examining a person's career over time. Support for work history analysis as a research methodology comes from a variety of sources in the social science field. For example, the work history technique can be used to investigate occupational mobility, analyse social class, unemployment, stratification and social mobility, the links between education and occupation, the immobility of labour, ageing and early retirement and on-going labour market issues (Dex, 1991). Work history information can generate both quantitative and qualitative data. For example, asking subjects to recall the number of times they have changed jobs in their working lives gives an exact number of job moves as a measure of labour mobility. Qualitative data is generated if subjects are asked to explain the motivations and reasons for undertaking these job changes. Further suggestions to utilise work history data include economists' interest in labour turnover and mobility, the analysis of learning differentials and pay discrimination, and the effects of social policies on labour market experiences and behaviour. Sociologists have an interest in changes in the nature of work, and conceptualisation of labour markets. This list is by no means exhaustive, but serves to illustrate the variety of uses for detailed and extensive employment histories (Ladkin, 1999a).

Given that work history analysis is a proven investigative technique used for studying many aspects of working lives, it follows that detailed career analysis can tell us something about how individuals build their careers over time. Career analysis is carried out by collecting work history data either longitudinally over time, or by using the recall method explained in Chapter 6. The information collected forms work biographies that contain information on all aspects of a person's career, for example, their educational qualifications, the number of jobs they have held, the length of each job, why they change jobs, and what the responsibilities were in each job. These work biographies can then be analysed at the individual level, or on an aggregate basis to illustrate general patterns and trends. It is from these general patterns that career analysis can reveal the dynamic of the labour market.

Labour Market Dynamics

Labour market dynamics refer to the structure of a particular labour market in terms of its characteristics and the behaviour which accompanies that structure. In a sense, what labour market dynamics describe are the moving physical characteristics of a market that determine both stability and change over time. There are common characteristics in all labour markets, and those specific to the tourism industry have previously been described in Chapter 1. In order to understand labour in the industry, the way in which the labour market behaves is crucial. The labour market is comprised of a number of variable characteristics which will affect the job opportunities available. For example, the number of jobs, the type of job, rates of pay, geographical boundaries, specificity of skills, size of organizations and required educational attainment. These structural characteristics form the basis of the opportunity structure of the industry. Individual career choice and opportunity is constructed by the nature and characteristics of the labour market.

Linking career analysis with labour market dynamics

Set against this understanding of career analysis and labour market dynamics, it can easily be seen that it is impossible to study individual careers without also exploring the labour markets. A career is, in its most basic form, a series of jobs arranged over time (Riley & Ladkin, 1994). However, there are issues for consideration at both the individual and organisational level that make a career more complex. At the individual level, a career is a concept which is central to individual identity (Van Maanen, 1977). As a person moves through his or her life, a range of experiences provide the raw material from which his or her personal identity grows. Given this personal side of careers, individual careers are comprised of personal choices, abilities and decision-making processes that occur continuously throughout an individuals' working life. These individual choices are the driving force behind career progression and development.

From an organisational perspective, careers are a reflection of the nature and workings of complex organisations and labour markets. In a sense, the internal and external labour market provides the opportunity from which career decisions can be made. This has particular significance at the beginning of the twenty-first century due to changes in work patterns, such as the increase in part time work, job redesign, job sharing and the changing demand for skills (Arthur, 1992). As a result of these changes, careers are altering in their shape and form, moving from traditional bureaucratic career structures that typically involve only one or two companies and few job moves, to those that are centred in the labour market, involve regular job changes and lateral job moves.

This interaction between organisation and labour market structures and individual human agency forms the total environment in which careers are developed and progressed. The internal and external labour market are the 'climbing frame' of career structures, and the way individuals choose to climb over the frame are represented by their personal choices and abilities (Gunz, 1988). This goes back to the importance of structure and opportunity as influential variables in career development. In the context of tourism and hospitality labour markets, high levels of mobility indicate an active use of internal and external labour markets for career advancement. For this reason, any career analysis to understand career progression in the industry must take into account the dynamics of the labour market. The example which follows uses the position of hotel manager.

The career paths of hotel managers

The role of hotel managers is an established one within the tourism industry. The notion of a 'hotel manager' carries with it a number of preconceived perceptions of the profession, and the people who engage in this type of career. Considerable attention has been given to hotel managers in the hospitality literature, which has provided some insight into the occupation and the people who undertake it (Ladkin, 1999b). The research presented here aims to illustrate the relationship between career analysis and labour market dynamics. In order to do this, three aspects of hotel managers' careers are explored, the rate of career progress, key stages in career development, and mobility and control.

Methodology and sample

The findings reported here are taken from an investigation into the career paths of UK hotel managers. A postal questionnaire was distributed to a random sample of hotel managers in the UK. A decision was taken early in the study to sample managers who worked in hotels of greater than 20 bedrooms. This decision was taken to eliminate the small bed-and-breakfast hotels that are dominant in the UK. This is not to deny the importance of this industry sector, but rather as the aim of the study was to examine career paths, it was necessary to capture the managers who had experienced mobility in their careers. Many managers or owners of the small bed-and-breakfast establishments have either worked in the property all of their lives, or had come from outside the industry. The questionnaire was designed on the principles of work biography, in order to provide a detailed career history of the hotel managers (see Chapter 6). The sample size was based on an assumed population of 6000, and on the estimating parameter of 'length of time to first hotel manager position'. The questionnaire was sent to 800 hotel managers, and with a response rate of 45%, and after adjustment for error, the actual sample size was 284. This exceeded the statistical requirement, and is therefore a statistically significant sample.

Sample characteristics

The sample of 284 UK hotel managers has the following characteristics. The dominant gender is males, who comprise 87% of the sample, with the remaining 13% female. In terms of marital status, 75.5% are married, 19% single, and the remaining 5.5% outside these two categories. The mean age of the managers is 40 years, with a range from 25–67 years and a modal age of 33 years. With respect to education, there is a dominance of hotel and catering qualifications within the industry, as 83% of the sample have specific hotel and catering qualifications. The remaining 17% have a general educational qualification not related to hotels or catering.

Rates of progress

One of the principle aims of the study was to try and ascertain how long it takes a person to become a general manager. In other words, if the position of general manager is seen as a career goal, how long can a person expect to have to work in the industry before achieving this goal? The length of time taken to reach general manager was measured using two different methods. The first of these was the *standardised* measure from the age of 18, and the second was an *unstandardised* measure based on the age the respondent first entered the industry after education. This was to take into account the different ages that respondents would have left education, the unstandardised measure eliminates education from the timeframe. The findings reveal that for the standardised measure, the mean length of time taken to reach general managers is 11.19 years, with a mode of 10 years. By the unstandardised measure, the mean age is 9.5 years with a mode of 8.5 years. By exploring the inter-quartile ranges of the results, the sample revealed a 'fast-track' of respondents who had reached general manager in 6.7 years.

This simple aspect of career analysis reveals an expected or likely time-frame of a career by providing evidence of rates of progress. This data suggests that a reasonable estimate for the length of time reach hotel manager would be 10 years in the industry. Taking this further, the next stage of career analysis is to try and ascertain what, if any, aspects influence rates of progress. To put it another way, is there a specific pattern of jobs, career decisions, or personal attributes that conspire to make one person's career progress more rapidly than that of another?

Key stages in career development

Knowing how long it takes raises the question of what the respondents did in terms of their job level and functional responsibilities *en route* to the general manager position. The purpose here is to try and ascertain if there are any particular stages of a person's career that are salient to career development. There are two aspects to explore in this context.

The first relates to the level of jobs that respondents undertake before they reach the general manager job. To this effect, the respondents were asked to recall their job levels since they left full-time education, to reaching their first general manager job.

The seven job levels are as follows:

Level 1 = Proprietor/General Manager.
Level 2 = Deputy General Manager.
Level 3 = Functional Specialist.
Level 4 = Department Head/Assistant Manager.
Level 5 = Department Section Head.
Level 6 = Supervisor.
Level 7 = Operative.

The biographical age distribution for the total sample contains career information for the respondents between the ages of 17 to 55 years. The biographical age distribution presented in Figure 8.1 illustrates the movement of the total sample through the seven levels of responsibility.

There are a number of observations to be explained from Figure 8.1 First, the total sample has reached general manager by the age of 49 years, with the youngest first general manager position being reached by age 28 years, and with 50% of the sample reaching general manager by age 30 years. Second, a small number of the sample began their careers in the operative and supervisory grades, and most of these respondents had passed through these stages by the age of 25 years,

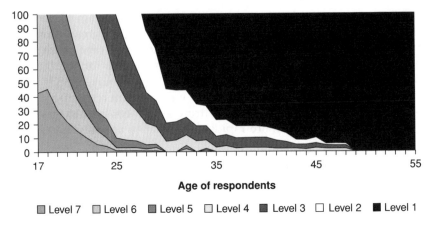

Age of respondents

☐ Level 7   ☐ Level 6   ■ Level 5   ☐ Level 4   ■ Level 3   ☐ Level 2   ■ Level 1

Figure 8.1 Biographical age distribution for levels of responsibility

although a small number stay at these levels until the age of 33 years. Third, with regard to salient career stages, the biographical age distribution shows the most salient grade prior to reaching general manager is department head/assistant manager (Level 4) as indicated by the width of the band. Second to this grade is that of deputy general manager (Level 2) and third, functional specialist (Level 3). As described in Chapter 6 the biographical age distribution takes the assumption that the salience of a grade is measured by the number of people who passed through the grade, and the amount of time spent there. It follows that the more people who spent time in a specific grade, and the longer they spent there, the wider the band will appear on the biographical age distribution. In this way, the width of a specific band in the biographical age distribution provides evidence of the salience of a grade in the career paths towards general manager.

To this effect, the biographical age distribution as a form of career analysis displays three key findings. First, that the assistant manager/department section head stage is a salient career stage. Second, the deputy general manager and functional specialist grades are also illustrated as being salient to the career paths of hotel managers. Third, the operative and supervisory grades are not key stages in the career paths of hotel managers. This suggests that the labour market recognises a pattern of job responsibilities that a person may pass through to facilitate career progression. In other words, if you have experience as a functional specialist, an assistant manager, or a deputy general manager, the chances are that over a period of time you will become a general manager. There is clearly something about these jobs that prepares individuals for the general manager job. These patterns are labour market signals in terms of preferred or valued career paths.

The second aspect to consider in relation to key stages in career development is functional responsibility. To this effect, the 284 respondents were asked to identify the functional area they had worked in for each job. Nine functional area were defined fore the analysis which were,

Function 1 = Overall Hotel Management.
Function 2 = Food and Beverage/Catering.
Function 3 = Front Office.
Function 4 = Housekeeping.
Function 5 = Accounting and Finance.
Function 6 = Sales and Marketing.
Function 7 = Personnel/Human Resource Management/Training.
Function 8 = Other (Hotels).
Function 9 = Other (Not Hotels).

The results are displayed in Table 8.1. Two sets of numbers are displayed, the actual number of respondents in each function in each job, and the percentage of the sample in each function in each job. The numbers at the bottom of each column display the total sample size for each of the job moves. As not all of the respondents have held eight jobs, the sample size declines as you go back in time across the eight job moves.

This analysis of functional job responsibility highlights four patterns worth noting. The first is the large number of respondents who have worked in the food and beverage sector on their way to their first general manager job. The percentages in the food and beverage function are larger than the others, and by the time job five is reached, the percentage in this function is nearly 50%. As indicated by the biographical age distribution, if it is assumed that the numbers of people who pass through a job is an indication of job salience, then clearly food and beverage is a salient job. This role is clearly important in the development of a hotel manager's career. By contrast, the low numbers of respondents who have spent any time in the functions of housekeeping, marketing, and accounting and finance is conspicuous. The suggestion here is that these are not salient career routes to general management. The third observation is that although not to the same extent as food and beverage, there is a high proportion of respondents who had worked in the front office and personnel functions although they do not rise higher than 20%. The final observation to note is that 5.6% of the respondents came

Table 8.1 Analysis of functional job responsibility

Function	Job 1	Job 2	Job 3	Job 4	Job 5	Job 6	Job 7	Job 8
1	284	206	144	102	69	45	32	27
	(100%)	(74.0%)	(52.7%)	(38.7%)	(27.9%)	(19.6%)	(16.5%)	(14.7%)
2		41	80	97	107	111	100	84
		(14.6%)	(29.3%)	(36.8%)	(43.3%)	(48.4%)	(49.0%)	(45.9%)
3		8	20	27	40	32	27	27
		(2.8%)	(7.3%)	(10.5%)	(16.1%)	(13.9%)	(13.2%)	(14.7%)
4		1	3	4	3	4	1	1
		(0.3%)	(1.1%)	(1.5%)	(1.3%)	(1.7%)	(0.6%)	(1.1%)
5		4	4	6	5	2	7	4
		(1.4%)	(1.4%)	(2.3%)	(2.0%)	(0.8%)	(3.4%)	(2.1%)
6			7	4	1	3	2	3
			(2.9%)	(1.5%)	(0.7%0)	(1.3%)	(1.2%)	(1.5%)
7		1	4	6	11	9	14	8
		(0.3%)	(1.4%)	(2.3%)	(4.4%)	(4.3%)	(6.8%)	(4.3%)
8		3	2	5	5	17	16	25
		(1.0%)	(0.7%)	(2.0%)	(2.0%)	(7.4%)	(7.8%)	(13.6%)
9		16	9	12	6	6	5	4
		(5.6%)	(3.2%)	(4.5%)	(2.4%)	(2.6%)	(2.4%0)	(2.1%)
Sample size	284	280	273	263	247	229	204	183

to their first general manager job from outside the hotel industry. This finding illustrates that it is possible to reach general manager positions with no prior experience specifically in the hospitality industry.

As with the levels of responsibility, these career patterns with regard to functional responsibility indicate that the labour market recognises the importance of certain functions over others for career advancement. The labour market signals indicate that the food and beverage function is where key skills are learnt that prepare individuals for the general manager's job. What career analysis reveals in terms of key stages in career development is there is an established career pattern, with some variation, that leads to the general manager's job. This pattern of job sequences is likely to be a function of individual choice and abilities, and the opportunities available in the labour market. As mobility is clearly prevalent in the industry in terms of career advancement, the labour market offers a range of opportunities for career development in terms of the level of job responsibility and the functional specialism.

Mobility and control

There are a lot of questions the surround the analysis of a job move. By examining the nature of each job move, career analysis is capable of illustrating mobility patterns. There are two main factors to examine in relation to job mobility and career patterns. The first is to examine the locus of control of career moves, or to put another way, who takes the initiative for job changes and career moves? The second focuses on the use of the labour market in job moves to test whether the job move involves the external or internal labour market.

The first factor explores the locus of control for job moves. In relation to the locus of control, two opposing propositions can be identified, which are first, that the *organisation* is the primary originator of career plans and career moves. Alternatively, the *individual* is the primary originator of their own career plans and career moves. The issue for career analysis is to test whether the locus of control lies with the individual or with the organisation. In many instances there is a mix of both the organisation and the individual who initiate career plans and moves, however, the relative strengths of these two alternatives are explored. To this effect, the research asked subjects to say whether each of their job moves was initiated by themselves or by their company. The results are shown in Table 8.2.

Table 8.2 shows that the total number of job moves generated by the 284 hotel managers is 1709. Of these, 1055 were self-initiated, and 654 were company initiated. This is 61.7% and 38.3% respectively, and illustrates the majority of job moves were initiated by the individual. The mean number of job moves is six. The career analysis revealed that within the sample there are individual variations in the ratio of self and company initiated moves. For example, 12% of the sample claimed to have initiated all seven of their job moves, and 2.8% of the total sample had all their job moves initiated by the company. However, the majority of the sample had a mixture of both. These results provide evidence to suggest that hotel managers engage in self-directed job moves, and are the primary initiators of job change and career development.

Table 8.2 Locus of initiative for job moves

Type of job move	*Number of moves*	%
Self-initiated	1055	61.7
Company-initiated	654	38.3

Table 8.3 Use of labour market for job moves

Type of job move	Number of moves	%
Internal	1083	63.3
External	626	36.7

The second issue in relation to mobility concerns the extent of internal versus external career moves, or put another way, how these job moves have made use of the industry. This goes to the heart of the debate on bureaucratic versus labour market orientated careers because it measures the use of the labour market. Table 8.3 shows the total number of job moves made by the sample in terms of within-company (internal) and between-company (external) job moves.

Table 8.3 shows the total number of job moves generated by the hotel managers is 1709. Of these, 1083 are within (internal) company moves, and 626 are between (external) company moves. This is 63.3% and 36.7% respectively. This finding is surprising, given that the majority of the job moves are self-initiated, as one would expect the majority of the job moves to take place in the external labour market. However, despite the predominance of self-directed job moves, the majority take place in the internal labour market, and therefore do not involve a change of organisation. This indicates the relative strength of internal labour markets, and suggests that internal labour market dynamics are influential on career progression.

In the case of mobility and control, career analysis reveals that managers are aware of their career options within their present company, and will make use of the internal labour market before looking outside to the external market. In addition, the managers are in control of their careers, and are usually the ones that initiate the job moves. There is a recognition in the industry that career progression cannot be achieved without mobility, as managers use the internal and external labour market as a vehicle for career advancement. With approximately 6–8 job moves over a 10 year period, high mobility rates are a key feature of the internal and external labour markets.

These three elements of a hotel manager's career; rates of progress, key stages in career development, and mobility and control have been explored in order to illustrate the relationship between career analysis and labour market dynamics. Further evidence of this relationship is provided in Chapter 14 and the use of personal career strategies by hotel managers in Chapter 12.

Conclusion

The nature of the relationship between career analysis and labour market dynamics is that they are interdependent. It is impossible to study and analyse career progression without taking into account labour market dynamics. Career progress is dependent on personal attributes, personal characteristics and dynamics of the labour market. Therefore, career analysis needs to examine what is happening in both the internal and external labour market, as well as the personal attributes and career decisions. Together these elements can illustrate how careers are progressed in a market led industry. By looking at general career patterns thorough the collection of work history data, career analysis becomes a powerful investigative manpower planning tool as labour market dynamics and individual career development can be revealed.

Chapter 9

Motivation and Occupational Choice: A Study of Orientations in Tourism

Introduction

In Chapter 2 we discussed the attractiveness of tourism employment in which one of the main issues of contention was whether it is the job or the industry which is the focus of attraction. The study that will be described in this chapter assumes that both concepts are salient to the decision on occupational choice. The rationale for this assumption is that all individuals have a particular 'generalised' attitude to work which influences many aspects of work, occupation and employment which includes choice of occupation. By generalised attitudes is meant a super-ordinate attitude towards work and living under which more detailed and specific attitudes are sub-sumed.

The traditional view of attitudes to work was that they are derived, on the one hand, from experiences at work and, on the other hand, from dispositional needs. In either case the assumption was that attitudes were derived from the individuals' psychological needs and their work situation. In an influential work, Goldthorpe *et al.* (1968) suggest that the values and attitudes exerted by workers towards work are in fact rooted in society. In other words it is the world outside the workplace, such as the family and the local community which largely determines the attitudes to work and not the role and tasks the worker has in relation to his employment. They called these 'large scale' attitudes to work *'orientations to work'*. The study is built on the seminal work of the valedictory studies.

Orientations to Work

To arrive at their concept, Goldthorpe *et al.* (1968) investigated an unprecedented number of aspects of working life, connecting it to social and political attitudes. The outcome of the study can be expressed with his words:

Until one knows something of the way in which workers order their wants and expectations relative to their employment – until one knows what *meaning* work has for them – one is not in the position to understand what overall assessment of their job satisfaction may most appropriately be made in their case. (p. 36)

Their empirical study suggested a three-dimensional structure to the meanings of work. These dimensions are:

- Instrumental.
- Bureaucratic.
- Solidaristic orientations.

According to their definition, an *instrumental orientation* means that work is seen as a 'means to an end' and where the purpose of work is to acquire the necessary income to support one's way of life. A *bureaucratic orientation* is when work is valued for its long-term security, a career and a steady increase in income and social status. A *solidaristic* orientation means that the purpose of work is not only economic but is carried out also as a group activity. Moral considerations sometimes receive priority over economic ones.

Later work has validated and enhanced the original study. Crompton and Harris (1998) confirmed that orientations are the product of structure as well as the work. Reed (1997) extended the original typology to make linkages with organisational commitment.

The appropriateness of this concept to the study of tourism employment lies in the assumption that working in tourism is more than just a job and implies a certain way of life (see Chapter 5). If true, then a concept, which simultaneously captures both work and 'life in society', would be suited to explain behaviour in that industry. In doing this, the concept might also say something about the role of job and industry in the general attitude.

Motivational Orientations in Tourism: A Case Study from Hungary

The data presented here are part of a study discussed in Chapter 7. What follows is the discussion of the way in which orientations to working in tourism occupations were explored.

For the development of the research instrument, we looked at the work of Goldthorpe *et al.* (1968) in relation of work orientations. Our study (Szivas & Riley, 1999) used that framework as a starting point but developed the original model into a four-dimensional model to suit the specific characteristics of the tourism industry. The proposed four-dimensions and the working definitions were as follows:

(1) *Instrumental utility*
     Tourism employment is perceived solely as a means to the achievement of economic advancement (exactly analogous to Goldthorpe's definition).
(2) *Positive commitment to tourism*
     Tourism employment is favoured for the intrinsic value of the jobs it offers, for example their image, the pleasant surroundings, the variety of tasks they involve and the potential for job satisfaction.
(3) *Refugee orientation*
     Tourism employment offers an escape route from a declining industry, an unpleasant job or even unemployment. For some, tourism is the 'least worst' option whereas for others it is seen as an opportunity for improvement. Tourism is seen as a contingency or convenience.
(4) *Entrepreneurial orientation*
     Tourism employment is appreciated for its suitability for one's private business or at least is seen as a potential avenue towards entrepreneurship.

In a similar manner to Goldthorpe *et al.* (1968), the orientations were not expected to 'stand in total contrast' but to work together in some rational manner.

Our main interests in exploring the orientations towards tourism occupations were:

(i)   To test the existence of the four dimensional structure of the motivational orientations.
(ii) To establish whether there are any dominant orientations.
(iii) To examine dynamics of the interaction between the orientations.

Methodology and sample

The primary data were collected through a self-completed questionnaire. The subjects were individuals who had *moved into tourism from another industry*. The definition of tourism workers was pitched fairly wide and included workers in hotels, restaurants, cafes, travel agents, taxi drivers, coach drivers and shop workers in tourist centres. In total

600 questionnaires were sent to a random sample of tourism workers in four selected areas of Hungary. The sample returned was 351, resulting in a 58.5% response rate.

The relevant part of the research instrument contained 30 statements measured on a five-point Likert scale. Each statement was designed to fit with the introductory words: 'I have chosen tourism because:'. The statements were designed along the four nominated dimensions of instrumental utility, positive commitment to tourism, entrepreneurial and refugee. To some extent, these contained the idea of push and pull model, the refugee dimension representing the push factor, with the other three proposed dimensions representing the pull factor. The proposed four dimensions and the relevant statements are summarised below:

Instrumental utility
I earned too little in my previous job.
I needed extra income in order to improve my living standard.
Tourism offered good earning opportunities.
I saw tourism as a profitable industry.
I needed extra money quickly.
I wanted an appropriate income.
I wanted to leave my previous job.
I wanted to achieve a better living standard.

Positive
I wanted better working conditions.
I wanted an interesting job.
I was attracted by the image of tourism.
I wanted to travel more.
I wanted to use my language skills.
I wanted a job that suited my education.
I wanted a job in which I could deal with people.
I wanted to work in a pleasant surrounding.

Entrepreneurial
It was easy to start a business in tourism.
My family had a business in tourism.
I wanted to accumulate capital for establishing my own business.
I saw good business opportunities in tourism.
I saw tourism as the most profitable industry for a business.
I wanted to establish my own business.
I have good business skills and I thought I could use them well in tourism.

Refugee

I was unemployed and needed a job.

The industry I was working in before was declining.

I did not see prospects in my previous industry.

I could not get a job elsewhere.

I needed a job which did not require any particular qualification.

The first job I happened to be offered was in tourism.

I like to try different jobs.

Study findings

The first step of the analysis included basic descriptive statistics, such as the mean score and standard deviations for each statement. The statements were then ranked which gave an idea about the motives In order to examine their relative importance, the 30 statements have been ranked by the mean score. The means and standard deviations (SD) for the 30 statements are shown in Table 9.1.

As Table 9.1 illustrates, this level of analysis suggests a strong positive attitude towards tourism employment. The statements with the strongest support were: 'I wanted an interesting job', 'I wanted to work in a pleasant surrounding' and 'I wanted a job in which I could deal with people'. What these statements suggest is that certain attributes of tourism employment such as variety, the physical work environment and the importance of interpersonal contacts are seen as attractive by those considering moving into tourism from other industries. The aim of achieving 'a better living standard' and 'appropriate income' also seems to be important.

Having obtained the basic shape of the motives for choosing a tourism occupation, the data were factor analysed. The approach to factor analysis was exploratory based on the four hypothesised orientations. The rationale for these factors comes from the review of the literature and from the preceding arguments.

The first step in the examination of the factor model adequacy was to examine the inter-item correlation matrix because without satisfactory correlation no factor solution can be expected. To this end, the inter-item correlation was regarded as a preliminary indication of the factor model adequacy where a high correlation indicates the existence of common factors.

Six items were found to be correlated at the 0.5 level. The variable pairs and the relevant correlation coefficients are as follows:

Table 9.1 Means and standard deviations for the 30 statements
($n = 351$)

Statement	Mean	SD
6. I wanted an interesting job	3.953	0.789
26. I wanted to work in a pleasant surrounding	3.880	0.688
21. I wanted a job in which I could deal with people	3.787	0.949
30. I wanted to achieve a better living standard	3.758	0.815
4. I wanted better working conditions	3.657	0.919
17. I wanted an appropriate income	3.628	0.860
27. I like to try different jobs	3.601	0.970
11. I was attracted by the image of tourism	3.570	0.965
10. I saw tourism as a profitable industry	3.506	0.847
5. Tourism offered good earning opportunities	3.474	0.890
18. I wanted a job that suited my education	3.409	0.987
20. I wanted to leave my previous job	3.381	1.052
13. I wanted to use my language skills	3.337	1.113
19. I did not see prospects in my previous industry	3.243	1.111
1. I earned too little in my previous job	3.184	1.056
14. I saw good business opportunities in tourism	3.066	0.917
12. I wanted to travel more	2.997	1.044
3. I needed extra income to improve my living standard	2.994	1.098
22. I saw tourism as the most profitable industry for a business	2.970	0.911
29. I have good business skills and I thought I could use them well in tourism	2.965	0.960
16. The industry I was working in before was declining	2.866	1.186
25. The first job I happened to be offered was in tourism	2.763	1.115
15. I needed extra money quickly	2.590	0.994
2. It was easy to start a business in tourism	2.557	0.849
28. I wanted to establish my own business	2.461	0.988
8. I wanted to accumulate capital for establishing my own business	2.413	0.940
23. I could not get a job elsewhere	2.263	0.962
24. I needed a job which did not require any particular qualification	2.257	1.058
7. My family had a business in tourism	2.234	0.965
9. I was unemployed and needed a job	2.182	1.091

14:    'I saw good business opportunities in tourism.'
22:    'I saw tourism as the most profitable industry for a business.'
       $r = 0.56$

5:     'Tourism offered good earning opportunities.'
10:    'I saw tourism as a profitable industry.'
       $r = 0.55$

7:     'My family had a business in tourism.'
8:     'I wanted to accumulate capital for establishing my own business.'
       $r = 0.52$

12:    'I wanted to travel more.'
13:    'I wanted to use my language skills.'
       $r = 0.52$

3:     'I needed extra income in order to improve my living standard.'
15:    'I needed extra money quickly.'
       $r = 0.52$

8:     'I wanted to accumulate capital for establishing my own business.'
28:    'I wanted to establish my own business.'
       $r = 0.51$

An examination of these correlations reveals that the statement pairs were in line with the hypothesised orientations. *Instrumental utility, entrepreneurial* and *positive orientation* are the ones represented here. The fact that the strongest correlation was along the hypothesised motivational dimensions is the first supporting evidence for the factor model adequacy.

The mean correlation between the items is 0.1322 which, given the relatively large sample size, is not insignificant. At the 5% level with a sample size of 300, the suggested significance level for the Pearson Product-Moment correlation coefficient is 0.11 (Child, 1970: 40). The fact that the average correlation and the majority of the items falls above this threshold encourages the application of the factor model.

Having examined the inter-item correlations, what followed was a number of specific tests to establish the factor model adequacy for the data. These were:

(1) *Bartlett test of sphericity* (3086.8090, significance = 0.0000). The large value and the small significance level indicate that, the hypothesis that the population correlation matrix is an identity matrix (i.e. that the diagonal values are 1 and the off-diagonal ones are 0), can be rejected.

In other words, the measure supports the notion that the correlation matrix has significant correlation for at least some variables.

(2) Kaiser-Meyer-Olkin (KMO) measure of sampling adequacy. According to Kaiser's (1974) classification, the computed value of 0.78747 for the KMO measure is close to the 'meritorious' category of 0.8 which supports the adequacy of the factor analysis method for the data.

(3) *Reliability analysis – Cronbach's alpha.* The reliability of the scale was of great concern. To this end, first the relationship between the scale and the items have been examined, followed by an investigation of the internal consistency of the test.

The internal consistency of the test is proven by a relatively high Cronbach's alpha of 0.8139 and standardised alpha of 0.8204. When applying the split-half method, the Cronbach's alpha from the separate parts are as follows: Alpha for Part $1 = 0.7557$ and Alpha for Part $2 = 0.6424$. Although these values are highly dependent on the allocation of items to the two halves, they still provide a satisfactory justification of the reliability of the scale. This provides further support for the application of the factor model.

Factor extraction and rotation

When selecting the factor extraction method, the relative merits of the two basic models (common factor analysis and principle component analysis) have been carefully examined. Principal component analysis has been selected for its ability to extract the minimum number of factors accounting for the maximum proportion of the variance in the data set (Hair *et al.*, 1995: 376).

It has to be noted here that the authors are aware of the fact that the method results in 'hybrid' factors where (especially in the case of the later factors) the unique variance overlaps with the common variance (Child, 1970: 44). Nevertheless, this approach was taken because the nature of the factor analysis is exploratory.

Orthogonal (Varimax) rotation
The Varimax rotation method has been chosen for its ability to minimise the number of variables having a high loading on a factor and thus facilitating the interpretation of the resultant factors.

Missing values
A pairwise exclusion of missing values was applied.

Number of factors to be extracted

In order to arrive at an optimum number of factors, several suggested criteria have been examined. As none is known to provide a single reliable criterion for the determination of the number of factors to be extracted, it was decided to examine and contrast the implications of the various methods.

Second, Kaiser's criterion suggests that only factors with eigenvalues of greater than or equal to one be considered. The importance of the criterion for our data is supported on two counts. First, it is considered to be particularly suitable for the principle component model and, second, the number of variables (30) falls within the region of 20–50, for which the criterion is most reliable (Child, 1970: 43).

The number of factors with a minimum eigenvalue of 1 is nine, suggesting that the factor extraction should stop after the 9th factor.

Third, according to the percentage of variance criterion, the number of factors to be extracted is related to the cumulative percentage of variance which they account for. The nine-factor solution suggested by Kaiser's criterion accounts for 63.9% of the variance. Following the suggestion of Hair *et al.* (1995: 378) regarding the acceptability of a 60% threshold in social sciences, the nine-factor solution seems to be justifiably supported.

The first task of the factor analysis was to find the underlying sub-structure of the data in the hope that factors would confirm the existence of the hypothesised orientations. The factor analysis used principal component analysis for the extraction of factors. The factor rotation applied was Orthogonal (Varimax). The analysis resulted in a nine-factor solution.

The nine-factor solution satisfies both Kaiser's criterion of selecting only factors with a minimum eigenvalue of one and the 'percentage of variance' which requires that the extracted factors account for a minimum of 60% of the total variance (Hair *et al.*, 1995). In our case, the nine factors account for 63.9% of the variance.

The naming of the factors did not prove to be an arduous task since the factors could easily be named in line with the hypothesised motivational structure. The properties of the nine factors together with their names are shown in Table 9.2.

Table 9.2 shows that each proposed motivational orientation is represented by two factors, serial numbers 1 and 2 were used for distinguishing purposes. For example, Factor 1 and Factor 8 both fit the category of instrumental utility orientation and were, therefore, named Instrumental utility 1 and 2, respectively. The ninth factor did not conform with any of the proposed orientations but could be easily interpreted as a 'drifter' or 'wanderer' approach.

Table 9.2 The nine-factor solution

Factor	Factor name	Eigen-value	% of variance	Cumulative %
1	Instrumental utility 1	5.50864	18.4	18.4
2	Positive 1	3.40147	11.3	29.7
3	Entrepreneurial 1	2,25554	7.5	37.2
4	Refugee 1	1.88157	6.3	43.5
5	Entrepreneurial 2	1.37529	4.6	48.1
6	Refugee 2	1.29750	4.3	52.4
7	Positive 2	1.26734	4.2	56.6
8	Instrumental utility 2	1.13772	3.8	60.4
9	The wanderer	1.04044	3.5	63.9

The resultant factor model can be best illustrated as a five-dimensional model:

- Instrumental utility.
- Positive commitment to tourism.
- Refugee orientation.
- Entrepreneurial.
- Wanderer.

The factors and the relevant variables are listed below:

Factor 1 – Instrumental utility 1
1. I earned too little in my previous job.
3. I needed extra income in order to improve my standard of living.
5. Tourism offered good earning opportunities.
10. I saw tourism as a profitable industry.
17. I wanted an appropriate income.
30. I wanted to achieve a better standard of living.

Factor 2 – Positive 1
6. I wanted an interesting job.
11. I was attracted by the image of tourism.
12. I wanted to travel more.
13. I wanted to use my language skills.
21. I wanted a job in which I could deal with people.

Factor 3 – Entrepreneurial 1
2. It was easy to start a business in tourism.
14. I saw good business opportunities in tourism.

22. I saw tourism as the most profitable industry for a business.
28. I wanted to establish my own business.
29. I have good business skills and I thought I could use them well in tourism.

Factor 4 – Refugee 1
9. I was unemployed and needed a job.
23. I could not get a job elsewhere.
24. I needed a job which did not require any particular qualification.

Factor 5 – Entrepreneurial 2
7. My family had a business in tourism.
8. I wanted to accumulate capital for establishing my own business.

Factor 6 – Refugee 2
16. The industry I worked in before was declining.
19. I did not see many prospects in my previous industry.

Factor 7 – Positive 2
4. I wanted better working conditions.
18. I was looking for a job that suited my education.
26. I wanted to work in pleasant surroundings.

Factor 8 – Instrumental utility 2
15. I needed extra money quickly.
20. I wanted to leave my previous job.

Factor 9 – 'The wanderer or drifter'
25. The first job I happened to be offered was in tourism.
27. I like to try different jobs.

The factor analysis supported the existence of the proposed factor structure. But it was of equal interest to the study to explore how the structure was applied. To this end, the raw data was re-calculated. The recalculation was based on the basis that the factor analysis now allocated the 30 statements to the nine factors. On this basis, by adding up the relevant scores for each factor for each subject, a new data set was produced. Every respondent had a score on each of the nine factors. The scores on the nine factors were then ranked and the interquartile range was computed. We defined 'factor usage' as being in the top 25%, which implies that a factor is 'in use' by an individual. This interpretation is arbitrary but rational.

In the context of factor usage the first question which arises is; how many factors did the respondents use? To answer this question, the

Table 9.3 The intensity of factor usage by the respondents

Factor usage	Number of respondents	Percentage of factor using sample (n = 258)%
1 factor	122	47.29
2 factors	68	26.36
3 factors	38	14.73
4 factors	20	7.75
5 factors	7	2.71
6 factors	3	1.16
Total	258	100.00

number of factor scores falling above the 25% cut off point have been computed for every respondent. The figure obtained indicated the number of factors used by the respondents.

It was found that 93 respondents (26.5% of the sample) did not use any factors while the remaining 258 subjects used one to six factors. Table 9.3 shows the frequency of single and multiple factor usage for the 258 subjects.

Table 9.3 shows that nearly 50% of the factor using sample is actually using a single factor. This is an important finding. What is also conspicuous here is the high occurrence of single and double factor usage in the sample, accounting for 73.65% of all factor usage. The question which naturally arises here is whether this conspicuous preference for a simple structure is supported by the existence of a few dominant factors. To this end, the single factor using groups were further examined. Table 9.4 shows the factor pattern of the group using a *single* factor.

Table 9.4 shows that *Refugee 1* factor is the most dominant single factor followed by Factor 9 which describes a *'Wanderer or Drifter'* approach by the respondent. *Positive 1* and *Instrumental utility 1* are the next on the list.

Given the fact that every motivational orientation is represented by two factors, the above table can be summarised by adding up the frequencies for factors representing the same *motivational orientation*. For example 38 respondents used the Refugee 1 factor while Refugee 2 was used by 5 respondents, resulting in 43 people who used a refugee factor. Table 9.5 shows the rearranged frequencies for the pattern of *single orientation usage.*

Table 9.5. shows that the most frequently used single motivational orientation was the *'Refugee'*, followed by the *'Positive'* and the *'Wanderer'*

Table 9.4 The pattern of single factor usage

Single factor	Number of respondents	Percentage of sample (n = 122)
1. Instrumental utility 1	10	8.2
2. Positive	21	17.2
3. Entrepreneurial 1	6	4.9
4. Refugee 1	38	31.1
5. Entrepreneurial 2	3	2.5
6. Refugee 2	5	4.1
7. Positive 2	7	5.7
8. Instrumental utility 2	4	3.3
9. The wanderer	28	23.0
Total	122	100.0

Table 9.5 Single motivational orientation usage

Single motivational orientation usage	Number of respondents	Percentage of sample (n = 122)
Instrumental utility	14	11.5%
Positive	28	22.9%
Entrepreneurial	9	7.4%
Refugee	43	35.2%
The wanderer	28	23.0%
Total	122	100.0%

orientations. *'Instrumental utility'* and *'Entrepreneurial'* orientations were used by the smallest proportions of respondents.

Conclusion

The factor analysis has shown that there is a structure underpinning orientations to tourism employment. The factor structure that emerges from the analysis is fairly strong and suggests that further research would be useful.

The evidence from Hungary suggests that in the observed period tourism was seen as a refugee industry. This is not to say that tourism is a 'refuge' for every tourism worker in Hungary. It is perfectly plausible to suggest that a considerable portion of the tourism labour force enters tourism professions as a first choice but what we suggest here is that tourism might play an important role for those who see their employment declining in other industries. For them tourism might be a 'second best option' but it might be one that evokes satisfaction and can also provide opportunities for advancement. The combination of the 'refugee' situation and the instrumentalism of the mobility as reflected by the motivational data might be an explanation for the general satisfaction captured by the study.

The question which naturally arises here is, that if people move into tourism as a contingency or because of lack of better alternative, will they stay there or will they move on at the first opportunity? Furthermore, the influx of labour from such a wide range of industries raises the question of how tourism itself is affected by this additional level of diversity. Clearly, in such circumstances it is as valid to talk about the adaptation and socialisation processes of the industry as it is to talk of training and learning. Newcomers bring with them experience which is likely to be very different from what confronts them in their tourism jobs. The literature on the psychological effects of the movement from production to service clearly shows that a considerable degree of adaptation is required. It is possible to suggest that the consequences of a labour force in the process of adaptation to service work is lack of service, wrong attitudes and lack of competence (Airey, 1994; Airey & Shackley, 1997; Riley 1997).

Chapter 10
Occupational Classification and Analysis

Introduction

To a large extent the tourism literature is concerned to establish the size of the industry in employment terms. This is important politically because it adds support to the economic value and status of the industry in the eyes of decision makers in government. Often tourism is conspicuously salient to a country's economy but in all cases tourism as an activity is part of an economy even if its contribution is not easy to see. The issue of definition and size has legal connotations particularly in areas such as industrial relations, minimum wage and migration. The concerns of governments are usually economic development, low pay, legal protection of workers from exploitation and how labour laws impact upon this particular industry. It follows that, if there is a concern for the people who work in tourism at governmental levels, then definitions of who works in the industry become important at the aggregate level (Belau, 1999).

There are two problems with estimating the size of the industry, first in defining the industry and then saying which occupations belong to it. This is not an easy task as the boundaries are not clear-cut. Hence most studies talk of 'related' occupations or 'indirect' jobs as well as those that are unambiguously tourism jobs (Heerschap, 1999). However, notwithstanding the issue of who works in the industry, there is also a concern, often expressed at the governmental level, about the levels of human capital achieved through training and education. A concern for the supply side and its quality is a part of strategic development of any tourism area or project. One perspective on skills and economic development could be simply to leave it to market forces operating though mobility and to companies to train staff to their own levels of competence. This approach assumes that a training capacity already exists within an industry. In this market-orientated scenario there would be little room for planning except at the corporate level. In reality such an approach puts power into the hands of large-scale operators who can influence the workings of the market. Governments and education departments would not have a central role. Quite another perspective involves the public sector providing the market with vocationally skilled workers. This brings to the fore concerns for educational investment and planning which in turn leads to an interest in the occupational structure of the industry for which education is being provided. What do they need to know? This concern for skills and knowledge presents its own problems in terms of planning and classification. Here the question is not who is or who is not in tourism but, whichever set of workers are the focus, how do we find out what they do and what skills and knowledge they need? Invariably an occupational classification scheme is needed.

The Inherent Problems of Classifying Jobs

If the relationship between jobs and education is important, and it certainly is in tourism, then ways need to be found that can inform both constituencies. There are inherent problems in this task that, for the most part, surround the notion of classifying occupations. To an extent, the accuracy and meaning of any classification can be judged by its intended purpose. In other words, the intricacy of a classification scheme depends on the use to which it is put. Sometimes crude schemas are perfectly acceptable. For example, some pay surveys use job titles only on the assumption that they are equivalent and yet produce results that are perfectly adequate for the purpose. However, the assumptions of equivalence have to be reasonable and based on some evidence as well as common sense. That said, even static profiles of jobs with appropriate qualifications attached are not easy to describe and always have to strive for equivalence (Guerra, 1994). The simple problem is that job labels which are socially useful information are insufficient for analytical purpose (Coxon & Jones, 1978; Reeb, 1959). Even job descriptions, despite their value in job evaluation processes, cannot capture everything about a job. The term chef, for example, can mean many different levels of skill and carry many organisational variables on its back. The job descriptions of airline cabin crew jobs can be identical but the jobs themselves, when investigated, may be found to differ widely due to organisational and external variables. Furthermore, *no job is an island* therefore to portray any job with out its relationship to 'all' other jobs is to sell the description short. The value of a good classification system is in its capacity to link jobs together in a coherent way that shows the differences and the rationale for the 'relative positioning' of all jobs.

The standard problem for any investigation of occupations is to find a way in which all the occupations under scrutiny can be brought together through a coherent classification system. Given that tourism itself is a broad church, any manpower planning exercise must anticipate a wide range of occupational titles containing considerable variation in job content within each job title. However, it must also assume that there is be a degree of commonality sufficient to categorise jobs within a unified coherent framework. Having stated the problem what follows is an illustration of an attempt to apply a classification process to tourism occupations *in order to illustrate the planning process*. The study described below, based on 153 tourism professionals, chose as its categorisation scheme a variation of an established occupational classification system that combines generic job content with organisational variables such as level of authority (Boehm *et al.*, 1976). The purpose of any classification scheme is to allow comparative analysis across job types and between job types and external variables such as pay, career path and educational input.

The Tenets of Classification Schemes

The primary analysis of jobs starts with four dimensions and these are:

- The work that is actually done (job activity).
- The level of skill required (job activity level).
- The level of the job within the organisation (job authority level).
- The specialised knowledge needed to do the job (job knowledge).

The relative value of these dimensions depends on the purpose to which the classification is to be used. For example a study of careers would certainly need a measure of authority level so that the trajectory of a subject's climb could be captured. Similarly, a job evaluation scheme would need a job activity measure as a check of the difference between jobs with different labels and between those of the same label.

Table 10.1 represents types of *job activity*. This set of categories has been slightly adapted from a standard managerial occupational classification scheme in order to make it accessible to managers in the tourism industry. It can be easily criticised but it is there as an illustration. Subjects were asked to identify their job with just two of the activities. This restriction automatically makes the description incomplete but does have the merit of capturing the real central activities of the job. In this way jobs can be coded by a set of signs – for example a marketing job might, on

Table 10.1 Types of job activity

A	Research and development
B	Conceptualization, planning and design
C	Operation and control of resources
D	Operation of plant / vehicles
E	Operation of administrative systems
F	Processing and transmission of data
G	Developing and care of natural resources
H	Provision of consumer services
I	Instruction and education

Table 10.2 Levels of job activity

1	My job requires a common sense understanding of simple procedures and instructions with only a general background understanding of the context.
2	My job involves defining and solving practical problems and determining the information required to do that, for which an understanding of how the whole operation works is essential.
3	My job involves tackling a wide range of intellectual and practical problems which requires an understanding of how the industry works.

this schema, come up coded as AH. Alternatively, an educationalist job might be coded as AI. They have a similar component so they are related but they also distinctive.

However, identifying the activity does not suggest the level of the activity. If, for example, a job comes out of Table 10.1 classified as AB that does not say anything about the intellectual level at which these two activities are pursued. This requires a job activity level dimension of which Table 10.2 would be a simple example. Table 10.2 shows just three levels of activity.

Table 10.2 is a fairly simple example but the underlying principle of delineation is clear. It is between common-sense understanding, understanding rational systems and understanding logical and scientific thinking.

As all jobs exist within a structure which, for the most part, can be represented by level of authority, then a dimension capturing this is essential. In practice this dimension determines the success of the scheme. For this reason it often requires a degree of research. The problem of

Table 10.3 Levels of authority

1	Operative level
2	Supervisory level
3	Assistant Department Head or equivalent
4	Department Head or equivalent
5	General Manager

Table 10.4 Results from the study

Job activity	No	Job activity	No
AB	31	AE	4
AI	28	FH	3
BC	14	CG	3
AF	10	CF	2
CH	9	HI	2
EH	9	IG	1
AC	9	BE	1
EF	7	CI	1
AH	5	EI	1
CE	5	FI	1
BH	4	BI	1

equivalence in jobs of similar authority can only be resolved through expert knowledge of the detail of those jobs. Table 10.3 describes the five levels of authority.

This dimension is crucial to the success of any scheme. It must reflect the difference in authority between jobs and be able to capture similarities of authority across a wide range of titles the function of supervision, for example, has many contexts!

As an illustration of what this type of analysis can produce, Table 10.4 shows the results for the 153 subjects based on Table 10.1. One of the purposes of the study is to see if these occupations share some generic content. Respondents were asked to identify just two activities from Table 1 that best described their current jobs. There are 57 possible combinations. Table 10.4 shows the distribution of the job activity levels across the sample.

Clearly the bias in the sample come out in terms of the prominence of research (A), planning (B) and education (I). However, one way to look at this data is to see it as 153 tourism jobs (93 job titles) 'reduced' down to 24 major activities. A disparate set of jobs with titles such as

Table 10.5 Classification by knowledge categories

Rank	*Subject area*	*Frequency*
1	Marketing (5)	61
2	Recreation and Leisure (10)	50
3	Business and Finance (2)	42
4	Economics (4)	27
5	Human Resource Management (7)	18
6	Hospitality Administration (6)	17
7	Urban and Regional Planning (17)	15
8	Education (8)	14
9	Geography (9)	
	Information Technology (11)	13
10	Transportation (14)	7
11	Sociology (15)	
	Psychology (13)	6
12	Anthropology (1)	4
13	Agricultural and Land Development (3)	3
14	Political Science (12)	
	Law (16)	2
15	Ecology (18)	1

Source: Churchward (2000: 63)

tourism development officer, conference manager, blue badge guide, director of a consulting firm and hotel negotiation manager have displayed a degree of commonality. This kind of measure does not attempt to comprehensively describe a job but does highlight its main components and this information could be valuable to educationalists.

The fourth dimension, and the one most closely related to education, is job knowledge. Here the planner has more scope to use appropriate knowledge categories. If the purpose of the classification scheme was primarily for education planning purposes for example, then academic subjects or disciplines might be appropriate. In the example displayed in Table 10.5 an adaptation of Jafari's 'wheel' has been used.

Table 10.5 shows an application of a slightly amended Jafari wheel to a random sample of 153 people employed in the UK tourism industry and who were members of a tourism interest group. Subjects were asked to identify up to two academic subjects that were important to their jobs.

Nothing too serious can be deduced from Table 10.5 except possibly that in this particular sample the business and commercial aspects of tourism jobs come to the fore. What it does illustrate is the diversity of knowledge that underpins tourism. If a researcher is interested in knowing the relevance of educational subjects to job performance or career trajectory then some kind of knowledge typology has to be related to as many job dimensions as possible to ensure the validity of the outcome.

The overall purpose has been:

- To illustrate the need for classification systems.
- To show that the diversity of tourism is not an insurmountable hurdle.
- To show the basic requirements of any classification scheme.

Conclusion

The rather simplistic scheme described above does illustrate that any job can be identified and have useful information attached to it. For example, the job of a consultant in tourism might have a job code of AB: 3: 5: 2.4. In other words, it would have research and planning as its main activities, performed at a high level of conceptualisation at the highest level of authority and requiring training in finance and economics. An alternative example might be a job in a hotel reservations department coded EF: 2: 3: 11.6. In other words, it would be concerned with systems and data processing, performed at a problem-solving level at a middle-management level of authority and requiring a knowledge of hotel management and information systems. The purpose of this information attached to jobs is for planning. If there is to be a relationship between education and work the information point between them is job content and collection of such information requires a rational classification. This illustration has shown how to find the generic content of a wide variety of jobs.

It is worth emphasising that the information is job focused not organisation focused and therefore allows for other organisational variable such as size to collected separately but used in conjunction with the job classification. This would certainly be necessary for career studies (Ladkin & Riley, 1994). Whatever the purpose of a study of labour however, the successful outcome will depend on the design of the job classification system. Because setting up a classification is time consuming getting the essentials right is crucial and these essentials are the four dimension described here.

Chapter 11

Skill Accumulation Patterns: A Case of Culinary Skills

Introduction

Of all the debates that take place within any industry usually the most ill informed one concerns skill. Skill is always surrounded by controversy because perceptions of skill are highly subjective and relative. Who is or who is not skilled is inevitably an issue. Nor is it simply a matter of debate because the assessment of skill is the strongest primary explanation of pay differentials. In macro-level economic terms, skill is always associated in debate with the rate of unemployment. By contrast, at the managerial level, there is always an issue of *'skill shortages'*. The fact that such shortages can exist alongside high unemployment often kicks the debate into ideas about cause and solution. In neo-classical economics the cause would be deemed to be a failure of market mechanisms but the solutions are usually seen as variations on increasing the quality of labour supply. What this usually means is more education and training. It is at this point that the concerns of industry managers and those of the economy as a whole may diverge because of two alternative objectives. Should a specific skill shortage which an industry complains about, whether quantified or not, be tackled or, should resources be addressed to expanding the skill base of the population as a whole (Green & Ashton, 1992)? Again, it not just a debate, national resources come into play. Solutions sought through education are constrained by finite resources so attention then falls on the next obvious solution; training. It is almost predestined for the debate to come up with strategies that automatically involve training. The paradigm is very circumscribed. Exhorting employers to undertake more training and encouraging education to expand its capacity are both worthy objectives but there is a case for attention being given to the other major training vehicle; the labour market.

The paradigm of education and training is incomplete in that it ignores the ability of people to learn skills and knowledge by mobility in the labour market. This incomplete picture tends to distort perceptions of the stock of skills available and the range of solutions that are possible. The literature on training concentrates on vocational education and on formal on-the-job training and neglects skills accumulated through job experience and job mobility. What such a narrow focus fails to appreciate is that skill has *latent qualities*. Skills can fall out of use but remain with the holder, they can become redundant but leave behind a capacity to learn new skills. People are not always aware of the skills they have and therefore cannot respond to market signals. Advocates of more and louder market signals need to address this issue (Adam *et al.*, 1992). These latent qualities are largely derived from experience.

There are many issues that surround the relationship between vocational education, training and job experience as alternative forms of learning. Such matters as the individual's costs, education resources, labour market dysfunction, and relative quality standards, are all implicated. What is clear however, is that these alternatives are not easy bedfellows and debate on their relative merits is common. Whilst it is never really easy to evaluate education or training, it is even harder to evaluate work experience as a learning vehicle. At an individual level such learning can be addressed under the 'development' umbrella, but how can it be audited on an aggregate level?

Rationale for Researching Skill Accumulation

Despite inherent difficulties of measuring or auditing experience and learning processes there is a compelling rationale to do so. There are three primary reasons for this type of research.

First, to make visible the useful learning patterns that can so easily be destroyed by the onslaught of change. Unknown to all, the baby can be thrown out with the bath water and then the cry goes up 'more training'! To appreciate the value of the argument that stable labour market dynamics are as important as change it is worthwhile examining the implications. The argument stems from the fact that often employment forecasts on tourism turn out to be wrong. Usually commissioned by governments, employment forecasts are an essential economic monitoring device. They are based on estimates of growth adjusted for technological advance but so often this factor is overestimated and compounded by an underestimation of the incentives needed to induce mobility. Forecasts have to use a static starting point but they must take account of the dynamic and stable forces within markets. The conclusion that many aspects of employment remain the same because they were still performing a function testifies to the overestimation of change. In this scenario, short-ages of skill can be the result of learning paths cut down by job change. The change may be perfectly legitimate but it may be that the previous job was a key one in a sequence of learning. If this were so, then the act of change has altered more than just one job.

Second, there is a constant interest in the relative performance of voca-tional education and learning by experience. There are numerous motives behind this debate. Whenever comparisons are made between education and experience more is known of the former than of the latter. It is possible to compare the performance of vocational education with labour market skill accumulation. The output of such a comparison would form the basis of a rate-of-return calculation, which is the normal way that educational feasibility is assessed.

Third, there is an advantage to policy makers to sample what is going on beyond organisational policies and practices. The advantage of sampling the labour market is that it goes beyond organisation-specific knowledge and skill and assesses the stock of human capital in a way that should be useful to the economic strategies.

Research Design

The empirical study of culinary education described here contributes to this debate by attempting to trace skill accumulation patterns. The study (Salleh & Riley, 1994) is built on the theoretical foundations outlined in Chapter 6. It illustrates that education and experience not only have different learning processes and time scales but may also have different career implications and qualitative output standards. Whilst education establishments and organisations concerned with food can, to a degree, control the learning processes and output standards of their craft students and workers, experiential learning in the job market is not controlled. Yet what the customer experiences is the product of dual and mixed learning processes. If complete control is not possible, can overall standards be audited? The study was located in Malaysia and compared the career paths of chefs who started with culinary education and those learning entirely through experience.

The methodology used here focuses on tracing skills as they add and acc-umulate. It is not a comprehensive method but does offer the opportunity for skills sampling and auditing across organisations and labour market sectors. If you ask a representative sample of companies what skills they have, they will tell you what skills they use. Ask the labour markets the same question and a range of skills emerges that are beyond current utility.

Locating Skill Accumulation Patterns

There are two models involved in skill auditing. These are the additive model, which measures brick by brick what people learn, and the development model, which regards changes of job to be key development factors. The assumption of the additive model is that whilst people forget skills, the variety of experience itself induces principles that can be useful. The assumption of the development model is that having learnt one skill it increases their capacity to learn more. It focuses on the difference between one job and the next and asks; what was new? The model used in the methodology described below is the additive model.

These are two components of this method, these are:

- The development of a template by a panel of experts. The panel of experts creates a 'ideal' pattern specifying what skills should be known and differentiating them into useful levels.
- The collection of work biographies, which focus on job experience and its setting and on job changes in the labour market. This task would require a questionnaire.

The first component lays down a validated standard to which the second component is compared. It is an ideal – actual perspective.

Creating a template

The first task was to create a set of skills associated with the target occupation, the chef. This was done through a combination of job analysis and consultation with practitioners and managers. In addition a small sample of workers were subjected to observation. As the Malaysian tourist industry is international in character there is a requirement on chefs to be able to cook western cuisine as well as national dishes. Measurement of the learning processes embraced both. From this process a range of skills emerges which normally exceeds what any practitioner actually uses because of variations within chef ranking. The output from this procedure was a set of 'dishes' that were cooked by chefs of different rank. At this juncture there was a lot of information but no order. To create order requires a template.

To create the template a panel of expert judges was set up. In this case the panel consisted of fifteen cookery and food experts including hotel general managers, food writers and culinary educator.

Each member of the panel was independently presented with a set of thirty cards each containing the name of a dish. They were asked to sort the cards on the basis of the skill content of each dish. The subjects grouped the cards and ranked them in order of skill. In this way, the judges simultaneously ranked the dishes and created levels of skill. For each judge the output is a structure of skill levels with specific skills located within the structure.

However, the judge's decisions cannot be used unless there is an acceptable level of agreement between them. This agreement concerns first, the placing of skills in levels. There has to be some concordance between them as to what skill goes in what level and how many levels there are. In such exercises a 'rule of thumb' parameter is 50% agreement. That is, only a skill that has been placed in the same skill level by 50% of the judges enters the template. However, more refined measurement is possible through the application of the Goodman–Krunskal gamma which gives a clear measure of association (Goodman & Krunckal, 1954; Knapp, 1971). This measure is based on the principal of relative similarity. It emphasises the tendency of two judges to rate the same two stimuli in a similar direction. It counts beyond exact matches. If when two judges consider two skills and one judge rates both higher than the other judge. This comparison is said to be similar because the direction is the same. If, they tie or judge is higher on one skill and the other higher on the second skill this is said to be difference. Again because the direction is different. The level of overall association should be at least 60% under this measurement. This procedure reduces the size of the template by eliminating items.

Once the data has passed these conditions the template is ready. It consists of a range of skill levels into which are placed named skills and pieces of knowledge. Figure 11.1 summarises the process by which a template is produced.

In the study of chefs the judges created a template of four skill levels with four as the highest and allocated the specimen dishes to these levels in the following proportions:

Level 1	4 items	(16%)
Level 2	6 items	(24%)
Level 3	7 items	(28%)
Level 5	8 items	(32%)

The degree of association in the matrix that produced the template was found to be 81% which indicates a high level of concordance. The proportion of cell similarity was 38%. The template, once created has two functions. It plays its forthcoming role as a comparative standard but it also 'hands over' its contents to the second component of the research design-the work biography questionnaire.

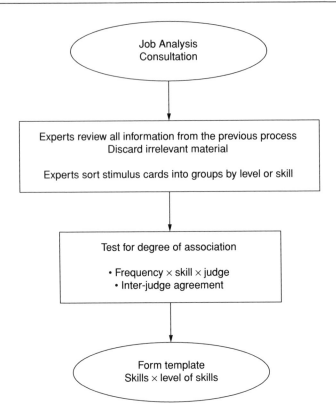

Figure 11.1 Creating a template

To make the template into a working instrument areas of strong disagreement were discarded. Borrowing the convention of the Delphi technique, which this method resembles, only a dish that obtained 50% support in terms of its allocation to a particular skill category was included in the questionnaire. This reduced the number of dishes from 30 to 25.

Creating a questionnaire on work biographies and skill accumulation

The questionnaire used was constructed on the principles outlined in Chapter 7 but contained an addition section on skill accumulation. The 25 dishes were listed against jobs and the subjects were asked if they could cook each dish. If the answer was affirmative, the subject then identified the place in his or her career, which could include education, where the dish was first prepared. This process links skill acquisition to career progression. Subjects are asked to indicate if they are competent in each skill. They are then asked to mark in which job they first performed this skill. The subjectivity may be checked against the job data. It may also be checked by random supervisor assessment.

The questionnaire was applied to a sample of head chefs, sous chefs and chef de partie selected randomly from hotels and restaurants across the whole of Malaysia. The sample size was 286. The sample split was, educated 128: non-educated 158. The distinction between the two samples was whether subjects had attended at least a two-year full-time culinary course. The output of each questionnaire is data on whether the subject could cook the each dish and at what stage in the career was the skill to cook that dish learnt.

Assessing the Level of Skill

In order to analyse the output of the questionnaire two processes take place. First, the template has to be aggregated to match the sample size and a time frame has to be fitted over the data.

Table 11.1 displays the distribution of the judges' decisions multiplied in proportion to the sample size. This expresses the allocation, for the whole sample, of the judgements of fifteen people. It forms the working template. The actual figures represent the sample's declared ability to cook the dishes, distributed by the classification set by the judges

Table 11.1 indicates that the actual distribution of skills matches the template reasonably well. In fact the difference can be accounted for by the fact that not all the sample knew all the dishes. The sample possessed 6080 skills out of the total of 7150 possible. This fact is not important. At this stage it is worth pointing out that Table 11.1 is not an accumulation pattern because it does not include a time frame. It is merely the sum of each skill level.

Table 11.1 Distribution of judges' decision in proportion to sample size

Skill level	1	2	3	4
Judges' distribution	1144	1716	2002	2288
(percentage)	(16)	(24)	(28)	(32)
Actual distribution	1091	1512	1665	1812
(percentage)	(18)	(25)	(27)	(30)

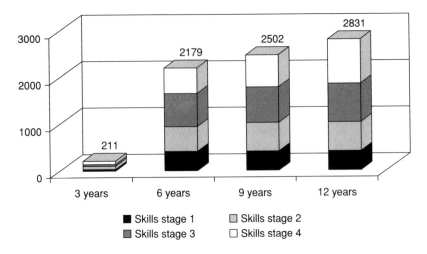

Figure 11.2 Distribution of skill – educated sample

An accumulation pattern requires a time frame. To this effect the early part of a subject's career was divided into four periods of three years each. This was done on the assumption that time as well as job would dictate what was learnt and on the common sense notion that most learning will be concentrated in the early years of a career. Some of the higher skills were learnt outside the period and that reduces the number of total actual skills to 5626.

Figure 11.2 displays the distribution of the four levels of skill over the four time periods for the educated sample as a cumulative frequency.

Figure 11.3 displays the same cumulative frequency for the non-educated sample.

In comparing Figures 11.2 and 11.3 it becomes apparent that movement in the labour market distorts the logic of the skill levels so that higher skills are often learnt before lower skills. It is noticeable that the earliest period contains skills from all levels even from level four! Perhaps more importantly there appears to be little difference in skill distribution between the educated and the non-uneducated samples. It might be expected that learning through experience would be more random and less sequential than learning through vocational education. This is not so here, both appear to be fairly random. The clear advantage of education is that a great number of skills are accumulated earlier. After six years the educated chef has more skills but the position evens out after that.

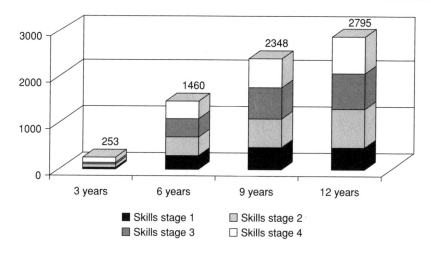

Figure 11.3 Distribution of skill – non-educated sample
Source: H. Salleh, 1995

Conclusion

The method advocated above been described as a way of uncovering a pattern of learning from the murky waters of the labour market. The underlying model was the additive model. It is reasonably easy to collect data for an additive model. It is a matter of gaining access to what skills a person knows, adding them up, and aggregating the data. The randomness of learning is shown by the degree to which skills cross levels and time periods against the prescribed pattern.

The success of this procedure depends upon the construction of a genuinely expert panel. In this sense the technique is closely aligned to the practice of benchmarking. It could be viewed as the investigative arm of a benchmarking policy. The success of the procedure is also dependent upon sensible decisions about what can be remembered about a learning process. Investigative manpower planning is not so advanced that it can, with certainty, judge what can be recalled accurately. However, experience does suggest that sequences are the key to memory and that if learning data is collected as part of a work biography then it is that much more likely to be reliable.

Chapter 12
Personal Career Strategies in the Context of Market Orientation

Introduction

It is one thing to locate the mobility patterns of aspiring hotel managers as Chapter 8 does, but quite another to find the motives which underlie those patterns. Any examination of the reasons why a person changes jobs at any particular time is likely to find any one or a combination of personal or organisational related factors. For example, a person may change jobs because they have been made redundant, they are relocating to another part of the country, they are promoted, they have been offered a higher salary elsewhere, or they desire a change of occupation. Within this pattern of job changes, it is possible that the individual is changing jobs for strategic reasons, i.e. they are actively seeking job changes in order to advance their careers. These strategies at the individual level are called personal career strategies.

Personal Career Strategies

Personal career strategies are the tactical manoeuvres that an individual may employ in seeking to advance their careers. They are closely related to career development, as they are the mechanisms used by individuals for career development purposes. Personal career strategies are comprised of three main elements; job search techniques, career planning, and personal attributes. These three combined elements form the basis of career development at the individual level.

Theories of Job Search

There are two main types of theory relating to job search techniques. The first set of theories is concerned with labour economics. In discussing the matching of people and jobs over time, economists recognise the individual cost incurred while choosing and changing jobs within and across firms. Micro-economists have regarded the job search process as a problem of decision making under uncertain conditions. Whilst the individual may have some measure of the probability of obtaining another job, less certain is the duration of the search. However, these models have been criticised as they have unrealistic assumptions concerning the search process. For example, they assume the individual is unemployed at the time, they assume the individual knows the probability they will find another job, and they fail to specify the process by which the search takes place (Arthur *et al.*, 1989). Attempts to address this final point have been to focus on the social networks that individuals have that may provide important sources of job search and career information, thus reducing search costs and uncertainty (Granovetter, 1973, 1974; Boorman, 1975).

The second type of theory is concerned with job search behaviours. Job search behaviour refers to the techniques and processes undertaken by an individual to look for a job, either in the internal or external labour market. This is often viewed as an information gathering process, both internally through a self assessment of personal skills, strengths, plans and interests, and external search that entails obtaining job and organisational information from a range of sources (Mihal *et al.*, 1984). The quality and quantity of information on jobs and labour markets is essential if the search process is to be successful. Stumpf *et al.* (1983) identify six components of the job search process which are:

(1) the source of the information;
(2) the method of exploration;
(3) the breadth, scope and amount of information required;
(4) the level to which individuals' energies are focused on the job search process;
(5) the confidence that individuals' have with regard to the success of their job search;
(6) the felt stress of the search processes.

Although labour economics relating to job search and search job-search behaviours have backgrounds in different disciplines, they should not be considered as diametrically opposed. There is often overlap from both fields in the job search processes. Job search strategies make at least two suggestions for individual career strategies. The first is that the potential search costs incurred by the individual in searching for a job either within or outside an organisation should be considered, before the process is embarked upon. In this way, the costs and benefits of the job search process can be assessed. Second, where possible individuals can use their social networks and personal relationships to obtain career information, thus reducing the costs and risks of the job search process.

Career Planning

In the context of personal career strategies, career planning refers to the activities undertaken by an individual to think ahead and to manage their careers. This is different to organisational career planning, which refers to the way an organisation will plan and develop the employees of the company. Both types are concerned with career planning, but in the individual context, it is planning activities that are lead by an individual. Career planning has be defined as a deliberate process of becoming aware of self, opportunities, constraints, choices and consequences. An all embracing career plan will identify career-related goals, and individuals will consider education and experience that are directly related to attaining specific career goals. The notion of a strategy is key to the concept of career planning, as is having specified career goals. Several authors have illustrated the need for individual career planning (Jennings, 1971; Bolles, 1972; Hall, 1976), and the career planning literature is dominated by three main themes. The first relates to the implicit need to plan a career, given the changing nature of working life, and an increasing reliance on individual-initiated career development, rather than relying on the organisation (Edmond, 1989). The second examines evidence to suggest that individuals who engage in career planning are more likely to be successful and with satisfied with their chosen careers (Hall, 1976). The third theme considers the variables which influence career planning. At the individual level, self-efficacy and locus of control appear to be crucial factors (Korman, 1971; Greenhaus & Simon, 1976; Gould, 1979).

Personal Attributes

Personal attributes relating to careers are more commonly discussed in relation to job choice – see for example, Holland's personality types relating to career choice (1985), and Schien's 'career anchors' (1975; 1978). Whilst career choice and career strategies are linked, in the context of career strategies, personal attributes refer to those traits that comprise a person's character. They may be tangible attributes that are valuable to career development, for example, educational qualifications or previous work experience, or they may be personality traits, including a person's self efficacy, self-esteem, and confidence. A person's tangible attributes (what they are qualified to do) and personality type (what motivates them) are two variables that will influence personal career strategies.

Market Orientation: The Contrast Between Organisational Behaviour and Market Behaviour

Given that personal career strategies influence career development, and are comprised of job search techniques, career planning, and personal attributes, it follows that a further influential variable is the labour market. The available labour market for job changes is comprised of both the internal labour market (the available job opportunities within the person's current organisation), and the external labour market (the market outside of a persons current job). As a consequence, personal career strategies always take place within either the internal or external labour market. An individual's career may be dominated by either internal or external job moves, however, in reality, there is often a combination of both.

This market orientation gives rise to differences in career development patterns, as individuals seek job changes in both the internal and external labour markets. Bureaucratic careers are essentially careers or job moves which are confined within single organisations. Traditionally, typical 'bureaucratic' careers involved job changes within the same company, and the organisation takes the responsibility for a person's career development. In the bureaucratic career, typically a person would join at the lower levels of a company, and work their way up through the ranks. In other words, Individuals follow well developed promotional lines. In contrast, since the late 1980's, the bureaucratic career has given way to some extent to the career that is developed in the external labour market, as job opportunities within the same company are no longer guaranteed. Individuals may have work roles which exist in different labour markets (Pike, 1994). As a result, individuals increasingly use both the internal and external labour market to advance their careers. It follows from these two contrasting scenarios that the locus of initiative for career moves will lie with the organisation in bureaucratic careers, and with the individual in self-directed careers which make use of the internal labour market.

Personal career strategies and their market orientation are best illustrated by the use of a example, which is provided here is the context of hotel managers.

The Development of Personal Career Strategies: The Case of UK Hotel Managers

The example used to illustrate this point is taken from a sample of 284 hotel general managers in the UK. Research was undertaken to examine the personal career strategies that lie behind a hotel managers' career. Personal career strategies were measured by presenting a list of personal strategies to the general managers, from which they were asked to indicate which strategies they had used in seeking to advance their career. These strategies relate to the three main areas of personal career strategies; job search techniques, evidence of career planning, and personal attributes. These were devised from information gathered previously in a pilot study that indicated likely personal strategies with regard to career mobility. Table 12.1 shows the list of 24 statements used.

The objectives of this instrument were first, to provide information concerning the ways an individual might look for a different job in both the internal and external labour market. Second, to ascertain evidence of career planning in both the short-term and the long-term and finally, to see what personal attributes are attributed as characteristic of hotel managers. Using a frequency distribution, the statements were ranked on order of importance. In decreasing order of importance, those statements that fell within the upper quartile range are as follows:

- always being prepared to relocate;
- trusting my employers that if I do a good job I will get promoted;
- not waiting to be told about promotion prospects;
- keeping informed of opportunities in the company through colleagues and internal bulletins;
- moving around to gain knowledge and experience;
- having clear long-term career goals; and
- always putting the career first.

The picture that emerges here is that hotel managers are very ambitious, have long-term career objectives, and are prepared to work within organisations to develop their careers. There appears to be a dual strategy at work here: to look for opportunities within the organisation whilst also using the external market. The willingness to be mobile in order to gain knowledge and experience for career advancement suggests the importance of adding new skills to the development of a hotel manager's career. The relationship between the need for mobility and career advancement is suggested.

Table 12.1 Personal career strategies

Statement
Regularly scanning job adverts
Regular circulation of my CV
Recognising the importance of chance opportunities in the market
Using contacts in the industry to get on
Keeping informed of opportunities in the company, through colleagues and internal bulletins
Trusting my employers that if I do a good job I will get promoted
Playing internal politics to help me get noticed
Using my family contacts in the industry
Not waiting to be told about promotion prospects
Always taking opportunities offered by company training schemes
Having clear short term career goals
Moving around to gain knowledge and experience
Always going for the higher salary
Having clear long term career goals
Using my college education in all my jobs
Continuing to take courses and improve my education skills
Having a mentor
Always being prepared to relocate
Being prepared to make financial sacrifices to learn
Being prepared to work abroad
Learning a foreign language
Always putting my career first
Emulating a successful role model
Keeping up a record of useful contacts

Finally, the personal strategies were examined by type, the division into job search techniques, career planning strategies, and personal attributes. Each time a respondent answered 'yes' to a strategy, it was awarded one point. The scores were added across the total sample to produce the total number of times each strategy was used. These scores were totalled for the three sub-divisions, and the results are as follows:

Job search techniques	=	794 (32%)
Career planning strategies	=	890 (36.5%)
Personal attributes	=	753 (31.0%)

Two observations can be made on these figures. The first is that the proportions of each category have very similar totals, indicating they are used with equal frequency, and second, out of the three categories, career planning strategies are used the most. However, the dominance is slim, only by a margin of 4% above job search techniques, and 5.5% above personal attributes. Although it is a crude measure, the instrument does serve to illustrate how the group of hotel managers used personal career strategies in their career development. Evidence of the three elements of personal career strategies is provided. For job search techniques, the managers are using internal bulletins. In terms of career planning, the respondents have long-term career goals, and are highly mobile. The personal attributes are ambition, shown by always putting the career first, and in actively searching promotional opportunities.

Conclusion

This exploration into the use of personal career strategies and their market orientation has a number of practical applications. First, it sends important messages to both organisations and individuals about labour market behaviour. By examining personal career strategies, they can provide information about how people use the internal and external labour market for their career development.

Second, personal career strategies send messages concerning recruitment and retention of employees. In the context of hotel managers, the implications for recruitment and retention are on opposite sides of a coin. On the one side, the willingness of hotel managers to be mobile and to use the labour market as a vehicle of mobility indicates that a hotel company could be reasonably confident of success if they wish to recruit from the external labour market. Hotel managers use both the internal and external labour market in order to advance their careers. On the other side of the coin, the opposite is true with regard to retention policies. Evidence from this study suggests that managers are prepared to make both intra and inter company searches for job opportunities, and that they place a high degree of faith in their employers. However, the commitment to long-term career goals suggests that if there is a high discrepancy between the career plans of the organisation and the career plans of the individual, then the manager will look elsewhere for career opportunities. More specifically, for recruitment policies, the research indicates the importance of labour market signalling and the need for advertising in order to indicate job opportunities. The research has indicated that few hotel managers bother to regularly circulate their CV's as a job search technique.

Therefore, companies must send signals to the market and advertise accordingly. With specific reference to retention policies, hotel companies would be advised to offer detailed and continual training programmes in an attempt to reduce the turnover of staff. The research indicates that hotel managers change jobs to gain knowledge and skills, and they are prepared to look outside the company for career advancement.

Ultimately, the examination of personal career strategies is a form of labour market exploration. In careers where mobility is dominant, as in the case of tourism and hospitality, it is essential that both organisations and individuals have an understanding of the internal and external labour market process at work in career development opportunities.

Part 3

Human Resource Development

Chapter 13
Human Resource Management: An Overview

Introduction

In Chapter 13, we turn to the issue of actually managing people in tourism and do so by exploring, in the context of tourism employment, the development of what is now commonly referred to, as human resource management (HRM). This area of management is not without its own problems, contentious issues and controversies but, notwithstanding this, we look at the main ideas and trends in the area to see how relevant and compatible they are to the particular context. Almost immediately Baldacchino's (1997) notion of the salience of the local context becomes important. Clearly the dichotomy between global and local in tourism is mirrored in a similar dichotomy between global HRM strategies and local conditions. This may be represented by the notion of size differentials – big company/small company matters in tourism employment. The two other forms of diversity that may also be important to employment relations are; who you work for and the industrial relations context. There is evidence of organisational diversity within sectors and within market segments and brands. Similarly, levels of unionisation vary by sector and by national industrial relations system with, for example the airline industry being highly unionised almost everywhere, as against the hotel industry where levels are low except in countries with highly legalistic industrial relations systems of which Canada and Australia would be examples.

Traditional and New Approaches to HRM

The generic literature on human resource management contains five conspicuous themes namely, the relevance of the function, the perceived recent change in character of HRM, the development of strategic HRM, the question of whether the changes are rhetoric or reality and the question of how feasible is *'trans-national'* HRM. That people are important and need managing is never in doubt but what is at issue is whether there is a requirement for an actual function within organisations beyond that is, fairly obviously needed administrative functions. The traditional view of 'personnel management' characterises it as reactive and, in the industrial relations sense, conflict orientation. Its role was conceived roughly as; get the right people from the market, do all the documentation and legal stuff and handle grievances and industrial relations problems when they occur. This is a maintenance view of the personnel function that sees it as necessary, but not really related to, the activities of the business. This description is simplistic and unfair but it does point up the contrast with modern ideas of HRM in which line management assumes greater responsibility for these functions and therefore becomes more proactive. In the proactive version the contribution of individuals is both sought and measured and is seen as part of the business itself (Beer and Spector 1985). It is this new proactive feature that has led towards the notion of strategic elements of HRM. Most notable of these are planning and integration with business strategy and planning. If, to this strategic view of HRM is added the international dimension, then arguments over centralisation versus de-centralisation enter the frame. The literature points to intermediary structures which come between the balance of power but suggest that a pure trans-national HRM strategy that ignores national context is impossible (Edwards *et al.*, 1996). The modern HRM movement changes the philosophy away from control and conflict to one of incentive and commitment. As commitment is essentially a psychological entity, the emphasis changes to an individualistic focus as against the group orientation of industrial relations models. These arguments are well reviewed in detail by Lundy (1994).

The rationale for this new approach to HRM lies first, in the modern need for organisations to both initiate change and to cope with it and, second, from realising that labour can be a source of competitive advantage. This last notion, it is suggested, has lead to the desire to gain more contribution from the human factor in organisations by developing human capital. However, the need for technical change requiring new levels of human capital suggests both an element of economic rationalisation as well as human development. Downsizing and re-training are odd bedfellows who are forced into marriage by new technology and the demands of market capitalism for enhanced shareholder value. There is real conflict here between the stakeholder models of HRM that exist to create sustained performance and the dominance of economic imperatives. This issue is represented in the literature by the dichotomy of '*hard*' and '*soft*' models of HRM in which the former emphasises the developmental aspects and the latter the economic imperatives (Legge, 1989; Truss *et al.*, 1997). The '*soft*' HRM models argue that sustainability requires commitment. The important implication here is that the workforce will be stable. In one direction, this argument leads towards the advent of a core and periphery employment structure and possible outsourcing (Atkinson, 1984). In this case, a core of flexible multi-skilled workers represents the idea of stability. In another direction, it leads to issues concerning the rate of change and the question of just how adaptable to change any workforce actually is.

Hand-in-hand with technological change has come the desire for organisations to be more responsive to changes in the product or service market. The desire for greater responsiveness to the marketplace and customer needs has led to flatter organisations and the notion of empowering employees. Whilst the former undoubtedly has empirical evidence to back it up (Kalleberg *et al.*, 1996), doubts remain as to the verisimilitude of the latter. Claims that it is essentially rhetoric and merely a device of senior management to control junior management carry some conviction (Hales, 2000). Possibly because there is less confusion over basic meanings, moves towards re-skilling, multi-skilling and flexibility carry more conviction.

What the debate on the nature of HRM illustrates is that all the fundamental questions in a business:

- how many workers are needed;
- the proportion of fixed variable labour;
- the proportion of added value available for wages;
- type of people the business needs;
- the type and range of skills needed

are in fact related to two fundamental strategy questions, which are:

- how stable should the workforce be and why?
- what is the rate of technological change and the range of its impact?

The first of these questions draws upon the issues of core and periphery employment, seasonality and other cyclic movements. The second part of this question has been argued out by the internal–external labour market debate which was referred to in Chapter 4 (Doeringer & Piore, 1971). The essence of this complex argument points to the specificity of skills, that is, the degree to which the skills, as the determining factor, are unique to the organisation. Skills specificity is, in turn, determined by technology and that brings the issues of the first question into the realm of the second. The rate of technological change determines the relevance of existing occupational structures and human capital. Revolutionary change, such as that experienced in recent years by the printing industry with the change from 'hot metal' to electronic printing, may radically change the nature of jobs and their skill requirements. Alternatively, an industry which experiences only incremental change, affecting only parts of its structure, may be able to simply retrain existing workers. The idea of traditional practice coexisting with technological change in organisations is not uncommon – education might be an example: chalk and computer living together. Diversity of skill levels is a common product of technological change so that people with high skills and those with low skills work together. For the most part it is the task of HRM to manage whatever technological processes throw up by way of diversity. Riley (1991) offers a strategic framework for capturing stability and technology.

HRM and Tourism

Although the idea of HRM being the same in all sectors of tourism is unlikely there are common problems faced across all sectors. Notable amongst these are first, the diversity of skill levels within organisations extending to the unskilled and the highly skilled in the same company. Second, the partial impact of technological change whereby technically advanced jobs exist with traditional roles. A casual look at the hotel industry for example would suggest that the main effect of information technology has been on marketing, reservations and financial control. Many fundamental jobs are only tangentially touched by technological change and even jobs that are involved with technology such as reception maintain the traditional role as well. There have been advances in food preparation, which have affected kitchens but not to any great extent in terms of roles. There may be fewer people in the cockpit of an airliner but things remain much the same elsewhere in an airline – people have to be served, luggage has to be manhandled. It is possible to speculate that the travel agency businesses will ultimately be the one most changed by technology. The point here is not that the tourism industry does not change it is that changes do not necessarily change the role descriptions of jobs and many jobs escape. The conclusion drawn is that managing a workforce in any tourism sector will involve designing policies and practices that embrace both high and low technology jobs which, in some cases co-exist in teams.

In one sense, technological diversity is just another kind of diversity like age or nationality but the question of how stable the organisation needs to be stands alone as being a crucial determinant of HRM. It has been argued in Chapters 3 and 4 that as demand is variable, productivity is a function of matching labour supply to that variable demand. Either through market mechanisms or union agreement some form of numerical flexibility is essential. In other words, the need is not for stability but a measured amount of variability. This in itself brings tourism employment into a degree of conflict with the assumption of commitment advocated by modern models of HRM. Can employee commitment co-exist with a degree of employment insecurity?

The dilemma for management is that they have to square the circle between needing employment flexibility and needing sustainable quality. The economic necessity of matching supply to demand in the short run has to share space in the thinking of management with a concern for quality. Managers have seen the link between quality and commitment and between both and a stable workforce (Arrowsmith & McGoldrick, 1996). New approaches borne out of these considerations have to incorporate economic flexibility with staffing continuity. The task is to bring market mechanisms in-house. In other words, create internal mobility through flexible working practices and multi-skilling. To do this however requires the organisation to secure an acceptable degree of overall workforce stability because without it, the task would be impossible anyway.

The literature suggests that the tourism industry uses three sets of practices. First, and by far the most important, is the drive towards simplicity and standardisation in services which lays the ground for labour substitution and consequent access to the general unskilled labour market (Kelliher, 1989). There is a hidden danger here in that this strategy directly attacks the intrinsic satisfactions which workers so value (Chapter 5). Second, they adopt the process of de-regulating job boundaries through budget constraints and organisational downsizing. Third, there is evidence that some organisations take a strategic line to flexibility through planned in-house training and tailored hiring policies. In reality the distinction between flexibility and mere coping with contingent events is not so easy to differentiate (Riley & Lockwood, 1997). It might be thought that the size variable would play a hand here in that one might expect it to be easier for smaller organisations to achieve flexibility more easily than larger ones. What evidence exists does not support this idea. Occupational identity is strong across organisations and acts as a barrier to flexibility. The key factors in achieving flexibility and commitment are training, and the patience and drive of management – good intentions – are not enough (Ackers, 1996).

Where organisational size does matter is in the level of administrative intensity. Clearly it is only the large companies that can afford a human resources function, however defined. This element gives larger companies the option – not open to smaller ones – of offering organised career progression. They also have the resources to move towards the developmental model of HRM where personal growth and training are strategies within the business strategy. What is less certain is the extent to which these developmental strategies encompass the entire workforce. Sustaining a managerial and technical capacity through succession planning, promotion channels and incentives would be in the interests of the organisations but extending down to non-managerial roles requires a specific rationale. In tourism the obvious rationale would be the high proportion of workers who deal directly with customers. Here the notion of *'supportive policies'* becomes relevant. In the area of customer contact, staffing continuity needs to be a clear goal of policy but to obtain that a degree of sensitivity to the demands of the role should infiltrate job design and supervisor ethos. Furthermore, modern trends in HRM suggest that staff are a marketing tool and firms use their performance as a form of comparative advantage (Szivas, 1999).

The issue of sensitivity of policy brings to the fore the problem of how far HRM policy and practice can or should reflect national culture. There are two cases to be considered here, first, that of managing a multinational workforce in one location and, second, of applying global policies to particular countries. The former is another form of diversity. The evidence suggests that acceptance of substantive terms of employment is largely unaffected by ethnic origin, however, the form and tone of supervision is strongly circumscribed. The second case is more serious in terms of its impact. Inward investment in tourism by multinationals has employment effects, changes the competitive conditions of local markets and in some cases can influence local industrial relations and labour law (International Labour Office, 1981). It is doubtful whether multinationals can directly change local labour laws but their influence is through *'best practice'* in HRM which may have an indirect influence. In truth, local labour laws represent local industrial history and culture and to some extent 'working within the law' implies accepting local culture. The influence of multinationals is through the political process and founded on bringing economic benefits such as jobs and training. It is this training aspect that brings multinationals into a relationship with national education systems. It is easier for a multinational to bring in skills from outside a country than to invest in local training and development. In developing countries multinationals can rightly claim that a lack of local skills will hinder the development of tourism. In this respect bargains are struck at the political level on the balance of importing labour and local human capital development. Part of that political process would be the extent of unionisation.

At a fundamental level unions are about controlling the price of labour and to do that they need to control the content of jobs. Bureaucratisation and unionisation share the same process. The scope of a job as well as its price is always the issue in both HRM and unionism. Tourism jobs are, in the main, not that easy to proscribe as many of them deal with customer contingencies – difficult but not impossible. However unionisation does not change the nature of the industry – it still has the same tasks to perform. The problems for HRM in a unionised context are to maintain the need for an element of instability in the workforce and to increase the scope of jobs in line with the need for sustainable quality. Evidence suggests that employment flexibility can be accommodated by collective bargaining agreements (Riley, 1993b) but that, in response to the other problem, companies pursue non-union policies where the system allows them to do so.

Conclusion

It is undoubtedly true that there are many traditional forces in the tourism industry that exist because of the largely unchanging nature of work in the industry. Of these, the ones that affect HRM are the rigidity of the occupational structure – particularly the differential value structure that maintains the relative status of jobs, the mobility of labour, seasonality and the constantly reaffirmed cost base of enterprises. In this last respect the assumption of feasibility studies by consultant companies in relation to labour inputs are constantly reinforcing the status quo. These traditional forces are maintained by the slow rate and partial impact of technological change which allows occupational identities to take root.

The distinctive problems for HRM in tourism are those of managing many types of diversity, of having policies that fit both the skilled and unskilled, having to balance centralisation with local conditions, being heavily involved in recruitment, having to achieve commitment from a temporary workforce and having to gauge a supervisory tone appropriate to the management of people who deal with people. These problems are not unique to tourism and they could be found, for example, in retailing, health care and merchant shipping. In terms of models of HRM the arguments suggest that, where it applies at all, the traditional model is likely to hold sway. The evidence in the case of the hotel industry is very strong (Simms *et al.*, 1988; Kelliher & Johnson, 1997; Riley *et al.*, 2000). Yet despite this the actual tenets of modern models seem in fact to be more appropriate to tourism.

To look at the problem of commitment and quality in a slightly different way, there is ample evidence of commitment, as expressed by intention to stay, in the tourism industry by a sizeable proportion of the workforce. Even at the unit level where labour turnover is most disruptive there exists a core stable workforce. The content of this core is from occupation right across the spectrum suggesting that what keeps people is not to do with the job but is context. Allegiance to the product and the team as the basis of organisational commitment has not been readily explored by HRM policies. Human resource professionals spend a lot of time on recruitment and selection because getting the right people, in an industry that works through people, is a base line fundamental. There is ample evidence of high job satisfaction but somehow that job satisfaction is not turned into commitment.

Chapter 14

Vocational Education and Markets: Tourism Education

Introduction

In analysing the labour market, a great deal has been made of the ease with which skills and knowledge can be acquired. To an extent, this misrepresents the true value of education in tourism. Many aspects of tourism, particularly management and planning, require high levels of knowledge. There is a clear role for education to meet these higher and deeper levels of knowledge required by the industry. Education is the major platform for the development of human capital for the industry. The intention of this analysis of tourism education, which in our perspective embraces hospitality education, is to take an overview of the subject. Our primary purpose is to examine two issues. First, given that vocational education is supposed to be closely related to employment prospects, what problems inhabit the relationship between tourism education and the labour market. Second, given that much tourism education is aimed at management, to assess what tensions exist within tourism education itself in relation to tourism and management. Such an examination may throw light on any organising principle that may inhabit the process of curriculum design.

Tourism Education

Tourism education, like any form of vocational education, carries the burden of having to balance three imperatives – the need to promote individual development, the need to advance knowledge and the need to be practical and relevant to industry. Sitting astride these objectives is the notion of employability. The question that always hangs in the air is whether these objectives are dichotomous. Both at the philosophical and practical levels vocational education is forever wrestling to reconcile them and therefore, by inference, the assumption is that they are.

Advocacy of a liberal education philosophy within tourism education is just such an example of this problem (Tribe, 2000). Given that the context is always one of finite resources, the fact that each imperative has its own set of needs which in turn, has its own constituency is a complication. It could be suggested that the academic community, within which there will be priorities and conflicts, represents both the needs of knowledge and individual educational development. Their role is to advance knowledge and develop students. Possibly a more serious, and certainly more contentious issue, is who represents the needs of industry in education? Is it particular organisations or prominent people or does the labour market speak for itself? If so, how? One interpretation of labour markets sending signals would be a kind of default argument in which validation of a curriculum is by the proven employability of the output of the process. Thus, if students get the jobs that were intended for them, all is well with the curriculum. On the other hand, industry representatives can speak for the market but in certain vocational areas such as tourism, where the market is so fragmented, such representation is itself contentious. In such circumstances, where there are multiple 'stakeholders', it follows that the structure of education and curriculum design will be the product of social processes involving power and interests. In a cursory and simplistic way the issues on vocational curriculum come down to two concepts – power and needs. Who has the power to influence curriculum and what are the needs and how do we know what they are? The two concepts become related by the notion of who defines the needs.

Putting aside for one moment the concerns of knowledge for its own sake, vocational education has to reflect the industry it is aimed at. Some response to the needs of industry is implied by the term vocational therefore there is always the problem of what they are. In crude terms, they tend to arrive under two headings – relevant knowledge and skills and sufficient numbers to fill job vacancies! Both concepts are difficult to determine, especially as the labour market is so dynamic and dominant. In order to explore the complications that exist in the employment–education relationship we raise four rhetorical questions.

Why teach what can be learnt by experience?

In the first place vocational education has to confront evidence, such as is displayed in Chapters 6, 8 and 11 that show that skills and knowledge can be accumulated by experience rather than through education. How far this process is actually acknowledged or used by education is not known but it does raise the issue of the correct use of education resources and suggests that this may be one of the benefits of better market signals, which can be incorporated into education and economic planning. In other words, it may be possible, through better *manpower planning*, to get a 'fix' on the point where experience and education duplicate. Such a point may suggest that certain areas of knowledge can be better achieved by work experience than by education or that experience is only beneficial if preceded by education. The continental European vocational approaches that combine apprenticeships and education illustrate the benefits of a clearer definition of what each can do. The effects of apprenticeships run through the whole structure of vocational education. Those very same skills that can be acquired by an apprenticeship are, to an extent, incorporated into vocational management education producing managers in the continental European model. This is management built on top of craft knowledge. In the context of hotels, this model leads to debates between industry and education as to the 'right' proportions of craft versus management. The general problem of understanding the relationship between experience and education could be enlightened by studies of the content of tourism jobs and by studies of skill accumulation patterns.

Matching educational output with jobs

In the first place, the shear diversity of occupations is problematic. Furthermore, the fact that within such diversity occupational labels do not convey clear messages (as the analysis in Chapter 10 confirms) only adds to the problem. To be honest, this is not uncommon in any industry but it is just that it is more salient where there are sectoral differences within the industry as is the case with tourism (Coxon & Jones, 1978). Previous research has demonstrated that trying to segment the tourism industry in terms of employment sectors and occupations is not an easy task (Airey & Nightingale, 1981; Medlik, 1993). The division of education into tourism and hospitality crudely represents the two major categories of jobs in the industry but it is not, and cannot be, comprehensive. Occupations such as conference organisers use knowledge and skill from tourism marketing, hotel management and many other parts of the curriculum. In other words the products of education are dispersed across all sectors of the market. A total overlap between education and job descriptions is unrealistic and probably undesirable in the light of progress and change. As the industry grows and changes new roles will emerge and old roles take on new responsibilities. For example, the manager of a historical attraction may need more than just historical knowledge. The role may, for example, encompass marketing, computing and media knowledge

Credentials and market signals

Although there are recognised qualifications in tourism the industry does not depend on them in the way that other industries such as the pharmaceutical industry does. This absence of credentialism has two important implications. First, it means that signals from the market are not easy to see and second, it affects the actual process of matching people to jobs.

The most useful signal from any labour market is the change in the levels of pay as an indicator of the state of the market and consequently of opportunity. However, complications occur when, as Chapter 4 illustrates, it is not easy to see the relationship between level of education and earnings. In such circumstances cost-benefit calculations on investment in education facilities are made that much more difficult. Such decisions are more likely to be made on some estimate of aggregate labour shortfall in sector employment.

The role of credentials in labour market functioning is two-edged. In attempts to encourage the labour market to work efficiently lack of credentialism is helpful in the sense that it reduces barriers for job seekers but is simultaneously unhelpful to recruiters trying to match people to jobs. Efficient labour markets benefit all participants and the skills and training of individuals are important pieces of market information but how that information is conveyed is problematic. Occupational titles are the commonest guide but, as has been expressed in Chapter 10, these do not convey everything or anything about the person. Occupational titles in recruitment are part of the structure of any labour market but they have the tendency to mitigate against change. New job titles can be created but people in the market may have needed skills but not the appropriate title. For this reason some governments have attempted to 'de-regulate' markets by training which repackages people in terms of 'bundles of skills' which are not attached to a particular occupational title but which are more visible in the market place. Such schemes give credentials to sets of skills which are accumulated through training with the hope that recruiters can see beyond occupational titles and beyond previous experience in particular job titles to seeing people in the markets as having 'sets of skills'. It is a kind of 'soft credentialism' which carries the intention of making markets work better. The UK 'general national vocation qualifications' would be an example of this approach.

The absence of clear signals also creates the opportunity for competitive interests to influence definitions of what is needed from education. Ingram (1998) showed how powerful corporate hospitality interests overwhelmed the more numerous small hoteliers in securing hegemony over a vocational curriculum. In this case management education won over the need for technical craft education. The competing needs of craft versus management are a sustained debate in the hotel industry. It is amplified by the issue of the role of food and beverage training in management education. In a very clear way this debate typifies yet another conundrum that of whether craft skill is more valuable than up-to-date managerial skills. Is knowledge of what is being managed as important as the skills needed to manage it? The evidence of Chapter 8 complicates the issue.

The fact that in tourism credentials are not universal currency is explainable by the fact that particular domains of knowledge are not confined within particular occupations as they are in many professions and manual occupations. In tourism, knowledge transcends occupations and is broader than the concept of the job. It is this aspect that leads to the third major headache for tourism education.

What to teach?

If vocational education has, in some way to be relevant and if, understanding of the context of the job is as important as its specific skills, then the ground is clear for a fight over what is meant by 'relevant'. One way to put it would be; knowledge of how the industry works versus what practical 'how to' skills are required to manage and work in it? To compound this dilemma is the perennial problem of the relationship between theory and practice. Tourism education, at least as defined by tourism educators, seems to favour the deeper and broader context of understanding of the phenomenon of tourism that involves theoretical frameworks from mother disciplines. Indeed the literature is concerned to show tourism as a subject area rather than discipline. This seems a superfluous argument unless it is followed by a justification for the rather narrow selection of disciplines actually applied. Geography, anthropology and economics seem to dominate with behavioural science conspicuous by its relatively small contribution.

In terms of the actual content of tourism courses, there is a continued debate about what should be taught and which disciplines should underpin the content of tourism courses. Obviously, the content of tourism courses is dependent upon a number of factors, for example, level of qualification, whether the focus is on education or training, or has a business or academic focus. However, it is the debate surrounding the *'core curriculum'* that is one of the most influential.

The idea of establishing a core body of knowledge for tourism has been debated for almost as long as tourism has been studied (Airey & Johnson, 1999), and the history of the debate is well documented (Airey & Johnson, 1999; Holloway, 1995). In the context of the UK, a tourism core curriculum is advocated in the higher education sector because of the diversity of courses in this sector. It is probably safe to assume that the desire for a core curriculum comes from educators rather than market signals. The core body of knowledge for tourism identifies the main subject areas that are considered important. This has been modified and developed over the years by a number of bodies, but most importantly, Burkart and Medlik (1974). The Tourism Society (1981), the CNAA (1993) and the National Liaison Group for Tourism (NLG) (1995). Airey and Johnson (1999) identify that these three initiatives provide the most commonly agreed definition of what is meant by a core body of knowledge for tourism. This is outlined in Table 14.1.

Taking the core curriculum identified by the NLG in 1995, these areas have been accepted as important for study by both academics and practitioners in the tourism industry. Briefly, *the meaning and nature of tourism* refers to definition, social and other conditions and determinants of tourism, and tourism motivations. *The structure of the industry* describes the interrelationships of the main component sectors of the industry and their operating characteristics. *The dimensions of tourism and issues of measurement* refers to scope, geographical knowledge and perspectives, patterns and determinants of demand and other resources for tourism. It also explores the sources of data and the management of information. *The significance and impact of tourism* examines economic costs and benefits of tourism, along with the social and environmental consequences. *The marketing of tourism* looks at the application of marketing theory to tourism. *Tourism planning and management* examines destination and site planning, partnership issues, and sustainable tourism. Finally, *policy and management* in tourism examines public sector policy, organisations in tourism, and visitor management issues.

Two themes emerge from the analysis of the core body of knowledge. First that tourism is a subject rather than a discipline and second, the perspective on management is at the industry level. The management of units does not appear as a strong feature. This is one area where tourism and hospitality part company. The disciplines that are evident are Geography, Economics, Anthropology and to a lesser extent, Sociology and Psy-

Table 14.1 Core body of knowledge from three initiatives

Burkhart and Medlik (1974)	Tourism Society (1981)	National Liaison Group (1995)
• Historical development • Anatomy of tourism • Statistics of tourism • Passenger transport • Accommodation • Tours and agencies • Marketing in tourism • Planning and development • Organisation and finance • Future of tourism	• What is tourism • Historical development of tourism • Determinants and motivations in tourism • Statistical measurement and dimensions • Significance of tourism • Component sectors • Marketing • Physical planning and development • Organisation • Finance	• The meaning and nature of tourism • The structure of the tourism industry • The dimensions of tourism and issues of measurement • The significance and impact of tourism • The marketing of tourism • Tourism planning and management • Policy and management in tourism

Source: Airey and Johnson (1999)

chology. The way in which all curriculum need to be analysed is in terms of how they secure the balance between an emphasis on business and on the tourism context. In other words, how the integration of disciplines is matched against the need for commercialism. The reality is that courses have to attract students and be viable in the commercial environment. Those with a vocational focus are more attractive to prospective students. This encourages tourism education to remain firmly as a vocational subject, rather than in the development of academic knowledge.

By contrast, the hospitality management education sector does incorporate the company and unit perspective and also clearly displays the struggle between skills and understanding of what is being managed. In this sense hospitality is no different from management education itself where the temptations to sacrifice the depth of contextual understanding for up-to-date relevance are supplemented by market encouragement to do so. It is not that the generic management schools lack depth it is that when faced with resource constraints they emphasise the more demonstrably useful managerial skills and techniques. If it is assumed that such techniques apply across different contexts then that automatically lowers the relevance of understanding the context. In support of this argument is the notion that the context is in fact always the same – business. It is one thing to state the arguments in very general terms but at the curriculum level there are contentious issues between business and management that invade course design. The fact that many 'hotel schools' are located in business schools is an indication that the industry is seen more and more as a business and in such circumstances subjects like strategy and decision making come to lead the syllabus.

There is no shortage of research that explores the trends and issues surrounding hospitality education, for example: Messenger (1991); Pavesic, (1993); Craig-Smith and French (1990) and Cousins (1992). Much of this research focuses on hospitality education provision, curriculum development, and meeting industry needs. A salient issue from much of the studies is the balance of a gradual move towards teaching more managerial skills rather than craft skills. For example, Cousins (1992) argues that if higher education is to prepare students for managerial pressures and skills, then the traditional concepts of operations teaching need to need reviewed. This view is echoed by Samenfink (1992). There are calls at broad level for the inclusion of more 'business' elements in the curriculum, in order that hospitality graduates develop strategic and financial skills. The inclusion of courses such as business skills and strategy, entrepreneurial skills, and facilities and personnel management are common components of current hospitality courses. There is a need for a broader-based curriculum which moves away from simple skills and practical training to general business skills and theoretical underpinnings (Pavesic, 1995).

Management education not only copes with having to be relevant but also, because 'being a manager' is conspicuously a role, it has to be demonstrably practical as well. There is a real risk here that the casualty will be the educational value of the relationship between theory and practice. It is a constant problem for management educators. Management is a social science and a direct relationship with social theory. Such theory has the function of explaining practice, critically examining practice in order to change it and legitimising practice. Theory also gives us methodology, the technique we use to compare theory and practice (Filmer, 1998). It is easily possible in the hurly-burly of management education for the value of theory to be mislaid. Indeed management education, at times, does give the appearance of having mislaid or abandoned theory in favour of techniques and moreover techniques which are decoupled, by time constraints, from their theoretical base. This may have been the result of an accident. In order to propagate the theoretical roots of managing and organising, management education detached itself from the activity of managing. The intention was to underline the principles of organising. However, the separation may have occurred at the level of the individual rather that at the level of ideas. As a result of this we have an emphasis on personal development, competence and transferable skills. In other words, analytical and critical thinking become absorbed into personal development to be achieved through application rather than through the initial grasping of principles and ideas that exist quite separately from their application. The medium for this type of education is the ubiquitous case study. The problem of reconnecting theory with both the action and context aspects of the practice through critical thought is time consuming and only works well with small numbers of students. Mingers (2000) gives an excellent example of how case studies can be used to fulfil the critical function of theory. There are two problems for management education in this sort of approach. First, the danger of education merely reflecting management practice and thus becoming simply simulation training and second, that it may run out of time and resources before it manages to get back to the depth. These are the dangers of case study teaching. No criticism of this approach is implied.

Conclusion

As tourism becomes more commercial, tourism education takes on the need to become more managerially orientated. This has two affects on traditional tourism education. First, it brings to the fore the issues of balancing detached analysis of the context with committed critical examination of performance and second, it embroils tourism education in the evolutionary change going on in management education. These debates within management education only become significant when they reside in hospitality education and where some degree of modular integration is deemed necessary with tourism. If tourism is rooted in explanatory theory and hospitality management in technical agency then the conceptual task for the student must be formidable. There are two areas of commonality that appear to be under explored. These are, first, the absence of behavioural science. This perspective of seeing both tourism and management as behavioural science would advance both. Second, it could be argued that hospitality education could do with a wider canvas and that tourism education could benefit from adopting the unit as a frame of reference. The outcome of both may be an increased depth.

Chapter 15
Planning and Development

Introduction

In Chapter 15, the sub-text rises to the surface in that throughout the book we have suggested that, in terms of planning, the tourism industry might be considered an 'awkward case' but one which can, none the less, be rescued if you employ investigative manpower planning techniques. Rescue is certainly the wrong word but our case is that manpower planning, particularly at the national or regional level can be usefully augmented by knowledge of behaviour. In other words selective and focussed studies can helpfully intervene in the normal forecasting and planning process. Furthermore the very awkward dynamics of the tourism industry make the use of such approaches more necessary.

Manpower Planning

At the macro level, manpower planning is essentially a statistic and economic activity and its functions are well described in its literature (Smith, 1976b). In terms of evolution the approaches have changed from, in the first instance, a belief in rigid forecasts to mistrust of such rigid *'blue print'* formulae and from such a position to move towards *'rolling forecasts'* in which revisions are build into the process itself (Smith, 1976a). Whilst welcoming this loosening of the process such flexibility does not sit easily with the resource allocation consequences of plans. The whole purpose of planning is to allocate resources and such implementation and application are usually long-term. This is particularly true of education resources – the decision to build a hotel school is a long-term commitment. However the real revolution in manpower planning came from the regular failure of forecasts and blue-prints. Again failure is probably the wrong word but the review of African studies by Jolly and

Colclough (1972) shows the deficiencies of the planning process – weak data, crude assumptions and methodological problems. Two strong themes emerge from this review, first, that as forecasts are dependent on projections of growth, what happens to the manpower element when the growth does not occur? Second, the assumption that education, given that it has the right capacity and the right incentives to direct individual choices, is often far from being accurate (Geo-Jaja, 1990). These deficiencies led manpower planning towards being more investigative and more behavioural so that it serves an additional purpose, that of, helping economics and planning to make more realistic assumptions.

The big leap for manpower planning was to accept that labour markets were dynamic irrespective of long-term movements towards equilibrium. Once this was accepted then it followed that an understanding of the dynamic processes, which involved both mobility and motives, were crucial to planning (Psacharopoulos, 1991a). This new approach pushed manpower planning towards looking for *investigative techniques*. At the same time advances were being made in organisational manpower planning which were developing as the size of corporations grew. This growth in corporate size drew systems thinking into organisational manpower planning (Bennison & Casson, 1984). The next leap was to realise that systems approaches could be used as a bridge between the particular recruitment issues and targeted sections of the labour market. Today corporate manpower planning is generally subsumed under human resource planning where figures and behaviour have a natural home. It must be said that despite changes in approach and emphasis, the basic tools of manpower planning remain the occupational classification and the age distribution.

In truth, the problem with manpower planning is that it works better *at the corporate level*, where it can more easily solve problems and be aligned with strategy, than it does at the national or at the small business level (Morris, 1976). *Yet these two levels really matter in tourism.*

At the heart of the planning process lie a set of individual decisions about which the process makes assumptions, and these decisions are made in the context of the labour market and the education facilities about which further assumptions are made. Even at its most statistical manpower planning is an inexact science reliant upon assumptions.

The important decisions are:

- Occupation choice.
- Choice to join the labour market.
- The choice to undertake full-time further, vocational or higher education.

- The decision to change job.
- The pricing of labour by management.

These decisions are further complicated both by being inter-related and by having resource consequences. In a very real sense, manpower planning and economic forecasting are concerned to best guess these decisions. The economic theories that surround them are concerned, on the one hand, with the opportunity costs of the decisions and, on the other, with how rational and information based the decisions are. In both cases the level of information and its influence are assumed. Whether individuals make decisions on the basis of alternative costs and benefits or follow some rationale interpretation of market prospects or both, is never clear (Williams & Leppel, 1994). Eklhammer (1972) displays a methodology that captures both the economic and psychological dimensions of the cost-benefit decision to go into education. It would, of course, be nonsense to suggest that planning decisions could be based on such individualistic data but knowledge of the dimensions used in the process is valuable to the macro case. Even if the micro case is put aside the value of aggregated behavioural patterns accompanied by motives is, that it presents evidence of what decisions have been made and why. If people are mobile, the question can be asked – what incentive can be inferred from the pattern?

The question of incentives is central to planning. The outcome of a manpower plan would be target numbers in various categories. To achieve such targets requires incentives. Such incentives in the form of training, education or special programmes would be based on an assumption that they are sufficient to influence occupational choice. In other words they can divert labour into the desired economic areas. That is essentially is how plans work – guiding people into occupations the economic forecast says will be needed. Yet if the dynamics of the market are considered then it must be recognised that incentives already exist and work in a particular way. People and their skills are already mobile in various directions which, may or may not be what the economy needs. Information such as pay differentials is crucial to planning objectives. This is the point where Psacharopoulos' (1991a) diktat – that we should know what produces the present is so important. At any one time a tourism industry has a level of quality, a level of productivity and a stock of skills. Some knowledge of how they came to be is an aid to improvement; hence our emphasis on investigative approaches. Part of knowing what produced the present is examining the performance of vocational education and its contribution to the quantity and quality of skills and the role of pay differentials as incentives to the direction of current mobility patterns. What moves people from one economic sector into tourism, between large and small firms, between occupations, into vocational education, between jobs and in and out of the market altogether? In this context studying mobility and motive together gives the planners some idea of what incentives are currently working.

The case of vocational education is complex. Given evidence that people can, with sufficient incentive, accumulate skills on the job, it could be argued that its role could be defined by giving it solely to the private sector. The problem with this argument is that it brings education closer both to the demand uncertainty issue and the insufficiently understood dynamics of tourism labour markets where fluctuations in the quantity of customers and skills would have adverse repercussions on quality of the latter. Perhaps the most significant role of vocational education in tourism is its role in terms of enhancing the quality of knowledge and skills at all levels. It is doubtful whether it can fulfil this role unless it is directed by some superordinate authority. Tourism vocational education has difficulty finding a home within the auspices of government. Responsibility for it ideally would exist in public and private sector partnerships, or at some point between the different stakeholder needs. However, this has proved impossible to achieve. Vocational education is an easy target for criticism, it is expensive and is assumed to create rigidity in the market because people so educated are 'fixed' to occupation (Psacharopoulos, 1991b; Watson, 1994). The defence against such criticism, from which tourism education is not exempted, is that such education has a direct relationship with economic performance, it is value for money and that it does not create 'fixity' in occupations (Moura Castro, 1987). It is noticeable that criticism of vocational education comes at the macro-policy level yet the response must come from the micro level and from evidence. The means to collect evidence is investigative manpower planning.

One of the problems of taking a holistic view of an industry is that conspicuous characteristics dominate over those that can only be seen at close quarters. Tourism has, to use the parlance of the hotel business, a 'front' and 'back' of house. Everywhere, across all sectors, there are customers to be served – the 'dealing with people' and all that that involves and, at the back, is a massive job of integration and co-ordination. Across both areas lies creativity, knowledge and a mass of diverse skills. Not only is the industry fragmented but also, the content of peoples' jobs also tends to be fragmented. Integration and co-ordination are everywhere and at every level, from the sous-chef bringing together a complete dish from the work of specialist chefs to a travel agent making a package of travel and accommodation arrangements, the need is always there. One view of job classification sorts jobs into *'dealing with people'*, *'dealing with data'* and *'making things'*. If this simplistic view were applied to tourism it would often find all three in one job. High-tech, low-tech and craftsmanship have to work together. It is possibly the feeling for wide scope that individuals sense when they think about coming into tourism. The encroachment of information technology will change some jobs radically and affect all jobs to a degree. More standardisation and specification is one possible road which may have some effects on employee motivation. One way in which information technology may benefit employees is in better demand forecasting at the unit level. Given the economics of tourism units, better forecasting means better employee management.

Conclusion

In the light of the above discussion on manpower planning, it could be argued that tourism is simply too complex and awkward to be addressed seriously. We do not agree. Given the growth of the industry and the importance of labour as an integral part of the service product and delivery, there is a clear need to advance our understanding of tourism employment.

This book has attempted to contribute to that understanding through two approaches: first, a broadening of thinking on tourism employment and, second, the use of investigative manpower planning techniques. These approaches have revealed insights at the level of the job, the occupation, the operating unit and the industry. Above all they have shown, not only that the macro level can be informed by micro-level studies, but also that human resource policies and tourism education can equally benefit. Tourism employment matters and there is a great deal of research still to be done.

Bibliography

Ackers, P. (1996) LeisureCo – Customer service, employee involvement and the flexible firm. In J. Storey (ed.) *Blackwell Cases in Human Resource and Change Management* (Ch. 16). Oxford: Blackwell.

Adam, A., Middleton, J. and Ziderman, C. (1992) Market based manpower planning with labour market signals. *International Labour Review* 131 (3), 261–279.

Airey, D. (1994) Education for tourism in Poland: The PHARE programme. *Tourism Management* 15 (6), 467–470.

Airey, D. and Johnson, S. (1999) The content of tourism degree courses in the UK. *Tourism Management* 20 (2), 229–235.

Airey, D. and Nightingale, M. (1981) Tourism occupations, career profiles and knowledge. *Annals of Tourism Research* 8 (1), 52–68.

Airey, D. and Shackley, M. (1997) Tourism development in Uzbekistan. *Tourism Management* 18 (4), 199–208.

Alpert, W.T. (1986) *The Minimum Wage in the Restaurant Industry*. London: Praeger.

Arrowsmith, J. and McGoldrick. A (1996) HRM service practices: Flexibility, quality and employee strategy. *International Journal of Service Industry Management* 7 (3), 46–62.

Arthur, M.B. (1992) Career theory in a dynamic context. In D.H. Montross and C.J. Shinkman (eds) *Career Development: Theory and Practice* (Ch. 3, pp. 65–84). Illinois: Charles C. Thomas.

Arthur, M.B., Hall, D.T. and Lawrence, B.S. (1989) *Handbook of Career Theory*. Cambridge: Cambridge University Press.

Atkinson, J. (1984) Manpower strategies for flexible organisations. *Personnel Management* August, pp. 28–31.

Baddeley, A. (1979) The limitations of human memory: Implications for the design of retrospective surveys. In L. Moss and H. Goldstein (eds) *The Recall Method in Social Surveys* (pp. 13–30). The University of London, Institute of Education, Sussex.

Baddeley, A. (1990) *Human Memory: Theory and Practice*. London: Lawrence Erlbaum Associates.

Baker, M., Mackay, R., Bishop, S. and Riley, M. (1992) *Costs and Manpower Productivity in UK Hotels*. National Economic Development Office, Tourism Society, London.

Baker, M. and Riley, M. (1994) New perspectives on productivity in hotels: Some advances and new directions. *International Journal of Hospitality Management* 13 (4), 7–15.

Baldacchino, G. (1997) *Global Tourism Informal Labour Relations: The Small-scale Syndrome at Work*. London: Mansell.

Ball, R. (1989) Some aspects of tourism, seasonality and local labour markets. *Area* 21 (1), 35–45.

Bartlett, F.C. (1932) *Remembering*. Cambridge: Cambridge University Press.

Becker, G. (1975) *Human Capital*. New York: National Bureau of Economic Research.

Beer, M. and Spector, B. (1985) Corporate transformations in human resource management. In R.E. Walton and P.R. Lawrence (eds) *HRM Trends and Challenges*. Boston: Harvard University Press.

Belau, D. (1999) Providing decent employment in the hospitality and tourism industry: The role of the ILO. *Tourism Economics* 5 (4), 149–158.

Bennison, M. and Casson, J. (1984) *The Manpower Planning Handbook*. London: McGraw-Hill.

Boehm, K.H., Farrand, M. and McKee, T.J. (1976) Introduction to IMSSOC. In D.J. Bartholomew (ed.) *Manpower Planning* (Ch. 9). Harmonsworth: Penguin.

Bolles, R.N. (1972) *What Colour is Your Parachute?* Berkeley, CA: Ten Speed Press.

Boorman, S.A. (1975) A combinatorial optimization model for transmission of job information through contact networks. *Bell Journal of Economics* 6, 216–249.

Bourdain, A. (2000) *Kitchen Confidential*. London: Bloomsbury.

Brinton, M.C. and Nee, V. (1998) *The New Institutionalism in Sociology*. New York: Russell Sage Foundation.

Brown, F. (1998) *Tourism Reassessed: Blight or Blessing?* Oxford: Butterworth-Heinemann.

Brown, N.R. (1990) Organisation of public events in long term memory. *Journal of Experimental Psychology: General* 119 (3), 297–314.

Brown, R.D. (1993) Meta-competences: A recipe for reforming the competence debate. *Personnel Review* 22 (6), 25–36.

Brown, P., Keenan, J. and Potts, G.R. (1986) The self reference effect with imagery encoding. *Journal of Personality and Social Psychology* 51 (5), 897–906.

Brown, D. and McIntosh, S. (1998) *If You're Happy and You Know It . . . Job Satisfaction in the Low Wage Service Sector (discussion paper 405)*. Centre for Economic Performance, London School of Economics.

Brusco, M.J., Johns, T. and Reed, J.H. (1998) Cross-utilization of a two-skilled workforce. *International Journal of Operations and Production Management* 18 (6), 555–564.

Burchell, B. (1992) Towards a social psychology of the labour market: Or why we need to understand the labour market before we can understand unemployment. *Journal of Occupational Psychology* 65, 345–354.

Burkart, A.J. and Medlik, S. (1974) *Tourism Past, Present and Future*. London: Heinemann.

 Burns, P.M. (1993) Sustaining tourism employment. *Journal of Sustainable Tourism*, (1) 2, 81–96.

Capelli, P. and Sherer, P.D. Satisfaction, market wages, and labor relations: An airline study. *Industrial Relations* 27 (1) 56–73.

Card, D. and Krueger, A.B. (1995) *Myth and Measurement: The New Economics of the Minimum Wage*. Princeton, NJ: Princeton University Press.

Castley, R.J.Q. (1996) The sectorial approach to skill needs and training requirements. *International Journal of Manpower* 17 (1), 56–68.

Cherry, N. and Rodgers, B. (1979) Using a longitudinal study to assess the quality of retrospective data. In L. Moss and H. Goldstein (eds) *The Recall Method in Social Surveys* (pp. 31–47). University of London, Institute of Education, London.

Child, D. (1970) *Factor Analysis*. London: Holt, Rinehart and Winston.

Churchward, J. (2000) A study of skilled occupations within the UK tourism industry (unpublished MSc dissertation). University of Surrey, Guildford.

Cohen, G. (1989) *Memory in the Real World* (Ch. 5, pp. 109–139). Hove: Lawrence Erlbaum Associates.

Cohen, G., Kiss, G. and Le Voi, M. (1993) *Memory: Current Issues* (2nd edn). Buckingham: Open University Press.

Cooper, C., Fletcher, J., Gilbert, D. and Wanhill, S. (1993) *Tourism: Principles and Practice*. London: Pitman.

Corcoran, J. and Johnson, P. (1974) Image of four occupations. *Hotel, Catering and Institutional Management Association Journal* June, 13–19.

Council for National Academic Awards (1993) *Review of Tourism Studies Degree Courses*. London: CNAA.

Cousins, J. (1992) Modern hospitality operations versus educational traditions. *International Journal of Hospitality Management* 11 (4), 289–292.

Coxon, M.P.M. and Jones, C.L. (1978) *The Images of Occupational Prestige: A Study In Social Cognition*. London: Macmillan.

Craig Smith, S. and French, C. (1990) Australian hospitality and tourism education: Current issues and future directions. *Hospitality Research Journal* 14 (2), 617–619.

Craik, F.I.M., and Tulving, E. (1975) Depth of processing and the retention of words in eposidic memory. *Journal of Experimental Psychology: General* 194, 268–294.

Crompton, R. and Harris, F. (1998) Explaining women's employment patterns: 'Orientations to work' revisited. *British Journal of Sociology* 49 (1), 118–136.

Cukier, J. and Wall, G. (1994) Informal tourism employment: Vendors in Bali, Indonesia. *Tourism Management* 15 (6), 464–476.

Cukier-Snow, J. and Wall, G. (1993) Tourism employment: Perspectives from Bali. *Tourism Management* 14 (3), 195–201.

Dex, S. (1991) *Life and Work History Analysis: Qualitative and Quantitative Developments*. London: Routledge.

Diamond, J. (1977) Tourism's role in economic development: The case re-examined. *Economic Development & Cultural Change* 25 (3), 539–553.

Doeringer, P.B. and Piore, M. (1971) *Internal Labor Markets and Manpower Analysis*. Lexington, MA: Heath.

Douglas, J.W.B. and Blomfield, J.M. (1956) The reliability of longitudinal surveys. *Millbank Memorial Fund Quarterly* 24, 227.

Drakopoulos, S.A. and Theodssiou, I. (1997) Job satisfaction and target earnings. *Journal of Economic Psychology* 18 (6), 693–704

Edmond, A. (1989) Building a bridge to a new career. *Black Enterprise* 19 (10), 96–100.

Edwards, P., Ferner, A. and Sisson K. (1996) The conditions for international human resource management: Two case studies. *International Journal of Human Resource Management* 7 (1), 20–40.

Ekehammer, B. (1972) Test of a psychological cost-benefit model for career choice. *Journal of Vocational Behavior* 10, 245–260.

Evans, D.S. and Leighton L.S. (1989) Why do small firms pay less? *Journal of Human Resources* 24, 299–318.

Fallick, B.C. (1993) The industrial mobility of displaced workers. *Journal of Labour Economics* 11 (2), 302–323.

Fazekas, K. (1995) A magyar munkanélküliség két jellemzö vonása I. rész. Munkatudományi Figyelö pp. 29–34.

Filmer, P. (1998) Theory and practice. In C. Jenks (ed.) *Core Sociological Dichotomies*. London: Sage.

Fitzgerald, L.F. and Lawrence, R. (1984) Autobiographical memory across the life-span. *Journal of Gerontology* 39 (6), 692–698.

Franklin, H.C. and Holding, D.H. (1977) Personal memories at different ages. *Quarterly Journal of Experimental Psychology* 29, 527–532.

Fuhrman, R.W. and Wyer, R.S. Jr (1988) Event memory: Temporal-order judgement of personal life experiences. *Journal of Personality and Social Psychology* 54 (3), 365–384.

Galton, F. (1883) *Inquiries into Human Faculty and its Development*. London: Macmillan.

Geo-Jaja, M.A. (1990) Manpower planning with occupational choice: A Nigerian example of mismatch. *Social and Economic Studies* 39 (3), 127–146.

Ghiselli, E.E. (1969) The efficacy of advancement on the basis of merit in relation to structural properties of organisations. *Organisational Behaviour and Human Performance* 4, 402–413.

Gittens, D. (1979) Oral history, reliability and recollection. In L. Moss and H. Goldstein (eds) *The Recall Method in Social Surveys* (pp. 82–99). The University of London, Institute of Education, Sussex.

Goldstein, H. (1979) *The Design and Analysis of Longitudinal Studies*. London: Academic Press.

Goldthorpe, J.H., Lockwood, D., Bechhofer, F. and Platt, J. (1968) *The Affluent Worker: Industrial Attitudes and Behaviour*. Cambridge: Cambridge University Press.

Goodman, L. and Kruskal, V. (1954) Measures of association for cross classification. *Journal of American Statistical Association* 49, 732–746.

Gould, S. (1979) Characteristics of career planners in upwardly mobile occupations. *Academy of Management Journal* 22 (3), 539–550.

Gowler, D. and Legge, K. (1970) The wage payment system. In D. Robinson (ed.) *Local Labour Markets and Wage Structures*. London: Gower Press.

Granovetter, M. (1973) The strength of weak ties. *American Journal of Sociology* 78, 1360–1380.

Granovetter, M. (1974) *Getting a Job: A Study of Contacts and Careers*. Cambridge, MA: Harvard University Press.

Green, F. and Ashton, D. (1992) Skill shortages and skill deficency: A critique. *Work, Employment and Society* 6 (2), 287–301

Greenhaus, J.H., and Simon, W.E. (1976) Self-esteem, career salience, and the choice of an ideal occupation. *Journal of Vocational Behaviour* 8, 51–58.

Greenwald, A.G. (1981) Self and memory. *The Psychology of Learning and Motivation* 15, 201–236.

Gregg, V.H. (1986) *Introduction to Human Memory*. London: Routledge and Kegan Paul.

Greve, H.R. (1994) Industry diversity effects on job mobility. *Acta Sociologica* 37 (2), 119–139.

Groshen, E.L. (1991) Five reasons why wages vary amongst employers. *Industrial Relations* 30 (3), 350–381.

Guerra D. (1994) *Occupations in the Tourist Sector: A Comparative Analysis in Nine Community States*. Berlin: CEDEFOP.

Gunz, H. (1998) Organizational logics of managerial careers. *Organization Studies* 9 (4), 529–554.

Hachen, D.S. Jr (1990) Three models of job mobility in labour markets. *Work and Occupations* 17 (3), 320–355.

Hage, J. (1989) The sociology of traditional economic problems: Product and labour markets. *Work and Occupations* 16 (4), 416–445.

Hair, J.F. Jr, Anderson, R.E., Tatham, R.L. and Black, W.C. (1995) *Multivariate Data Analysis* (4th edn). London: Prentice-Hall.

Hales, C. (2000) Management and empowerment programmes. *Work, Employment and Society* 14 (3), 501–519.

Hall, D.T. (1976) *Careers in Organsiations*. Pacific Palisades, CA: Goodyear.

Hecht, J.J. (1980) *The Domestic Servant in Eighteenth-Century England*. London: Routledge and Kegan Paul.

Heerschap, N. (1999) The employment module for the tourism satellite account of the OECD. *Tourism Economics* 5 (4), 383–413.

Hobcraft J., Menkin, J. and Preston, S. (1982) Age, period and cohort analysis in demography: A review. *Population Index* 48 (1), 4–43.

Hochschild, A.R. (1983) *The Managed Heart: The Commercialization of Human Feeling*. Berkeley, CA: University of California Press.

Holland, J.L. (1985) *Making Vocational Choices: Theory of Careers* (2nd edn). Englewood Cliffs, NJ: Prentice Hall.

Holloway, J. (1995) *Towards a Core Curriculum for Tourism* (discussion paper). London: National Liaison Group.

Holman, D. (2000) Contemporary models of management education in the UK. *Management Learning* 31 (2), 196–216.

Homans, G. (1962) *Sentiments and Activities*. London: Routledge and Kegan Paul.

Howes, J.L. and Katz, A.N. (1992) Remote memory: Recalling autobiographical and public events from across the lifespan. *Canadian Journal of Psychology* 46 (1), 92–116.

Huttenlocher. J., Hedges, L.V. and Bradburn, N.M. (1990) Reports of elapsed time: Bounding and rounding processes in estimation. *Journal of Experimental Psychology: Learning, Memory and Cognition* 16, 196–213.

Huttenlocher, J., Hedges, L.V. and Prohaska, V. (1988) Hierarchical organization in ordered domains: Estimating the dates of events. *Psychological Review* 95 (4), 471–484.

Hyman, R. and Brough, I. (1975) Social values and industrial relations. *International Journal of Manpower* 14 (1), 34–39.

Ingram, P. (1998) Changing the rules: Interests, organizations, and institutional change in the US hospitality industry. In M.C. Brinton and V. Nee (eds) *The New Institutionalism in Sociology*. New York: Russell Sage Foundation.

International Labour Office (1981) *Employment Effects of Multinational Enterprises in Developing Countries*. Geneva: International Labour Office.

International Labour Office, Hotel, Catering and Tourism Committee (1989a) *General Report*. Geneva: International Labour Office.

International Labour Office, Hotel, Catering and Tourism Committee (1989b) *Productivity and Training in the Hotel, Catering and Tourism Sector*. Geneva: International Labour Office.

Jafari, J. (1977) Editor's page. *Annals of Tourism Research* Oct./Dec., 5, 6–11.

Jafari, J., Pizam, A. and Przeclawski, K. (1990) A sociolocultural study of tourism as a factor of change. *Annals of Tourism Research* 17 (3), 469–472.

Jennings, E.E. (1971) *Routes to the Executive Suite*. New York: Macmillan.

Jolly, R. and Colclough, C. (1972) African manpower plans: An evaluation. *International Labor Review* August–September, 106, 207-264.

Kalleberg, A.L., Knoke, D., Narsden, P.V. and Spaeth, J.L. (1996) *Organisations in America: Analysing their Structures and Human Resource Practices*. London: Sage.

Keenan, J.M. and Baillet, S.D. (1980) Memory for personality and socially significant events. In G.A. Keeney, R.W. Morgan and K.K. Ray (1980) The Camel model: A model of career planning in a hierarchy. In A.R. Smith (ed.) *Corporate Manpower Planning* (pp. 112–126). Aldershot: Gower.

Kelliher, C. (1989) Flexibility in employment: Developments in the hospitality industry. *International Journal of Hospitality Management* 8 (2), 57–166.

Kelliher, C. and Johnson, K. (1997) Personnel management in hotels – an update: A move to human resource management?' *Progress in Tourism and Hospitality Research* 4 (4), 321–332.

Knapp, T.R. (1971) *Statistics for Educational Measurement* (Ch. 4). London: Intext Educational Publishers.

Korman, A.K. (1971) *Industrial and Organizational Psychology*. Englewood Cliffs, NJ: Prentice Hall.

Ladkin, A. (1999a) Life and work history analysis: The value of this research method for hospitality and tourism. *Tourism Management* 20, 37–45.

Ladkin, A. (1999b) Hotel general managers: A review of prominent research themes. *International Journal of Tourism Research* 1 (3), 167–193.

Ladkin, A. and Riley, M. (1994a) A research update. *Tourism Management* 15 (3), 221–222.

Ladkin, A. and Riley, M. (1994b) Career theory and tourism. In *Progress in Tourism, Recreation and Hospitality Management* (6, pp. 225–237). Chichester: Wiley.

Ladkin, A. and Riley, M. (1996) Mobility and structure in the career path of UK hotel managers: A labour market hybrid of the bureaucratic model? *Tourism Management* 17 (6), 443–452.

Lam, A. (2000) Tacit knowledge, organizational learning and societal institutions: An integrated framework. *Organization Studies* 21 (3), 487–513.

Larsen, S.F. (1988) Remembering without experiencing: Memory for reported events. In U. Neisser and E. Winograd (eds) *Remembering Reconsidered: Ecological and Traditional Approaches to Memory* (pp. 326–355). Cambridge: Cambridge University Press.

Legge K. (1989) Human resource management: A critical analysis. In J. Storey (ed.) *New Perspectives in Human Resource Management*. London: Routledge.

Leiper, N. (1979) The framework of tourism: Towards a definition of tourism, tourist, and the tourist industry. *Annals of Tourism Research* 6 (4), 390–407.

Lilien, D. (1982) Sectoral shifts and cyclical unemployment. *Journal of Political Economy* 90, 777–793.

Linton, M. (1986) Ways of searching and the contents of memory. In D.C. Rubin (ed.) *Autobiographical Memory* (pp. 50–67). Cambridge: Cambridge University Press.

Lundy, O. (1994) From personnel management to strategic human resource management. *International Journal of Human Resource Management* 5 (3) 687–719.

Maillat, D. (1984) Mobiltiy channels: An instrument for analysing and regulating the local labour market. *International Labour Review* 123 (3), 349–362.

Mallier, T. and Shafto, T. (1989) *The Economics of Labour Markets and Management*. London: Hutchinson.

Makin, P., Cooper, C. and Cox, C. (1996) *Organizations and the Psychological Contract*. Leicester: BPS Books.

Marin, B. and Mayntz, R. (1991) (eds) *Policy Networks*. Campus Verlag: Westview Press.

Markus, H. (1977) Self-schemata and processing information about the self. *Journal of Personality and Social Psychology* 35 (2), 63–78.

Mars, G., Bryant, D. and Mitchell, P. (1979) *Manpower Problems in the Hotel and Catering Industry*. Farnborough: Gower.

Mathieson, A. and Wall, G. (1982) *Tourism: Economic, Physical and Social Impacts*. Harlow: Longman.

Matlin, M. and Stang, D. (1978) *The Pollyannapricipal: Selectivity in Language, Memory and Thought*. Cambridge, MA: Schenkman.

McCormak, P.D. (1979) Autobiographical memory in the aged. *Canadian Journal of Psychology* 33, 118–124.

Medlik, S. (1993) *The Study of Tourism*. Warsaw Institute, Warsaw, Poland.

Messenger, S. (1991) The UK hospitality and tourism industry: An overview of the issues affecting the supply of education and training in the 1990s. *Progress in Tourism, Recreation and Hospitality Management* 3, 247–263.

Mihal, W.L., Source, P.A. and Comte, T.E. (1984) A process model of individual careers decision making. *Academy of Management Review* 9, 95–103.

Mincer, J. and Jovanovic, B. (1981) Labor mobility and wages. In S. Rosen (ed.) *Studies in Labor Markets*. Chicago: University of Chicago Press.

Mingers, J. (2000) What is it to be critical? Teaching a critical approach to management undergraduates. *Management Learning* 31 (2), 221–236.

Morris, B.R. (1976) An appreciation of manpower planning. In D. Bartholomew (ed.) *Manpower Planning* (Ch. 3). Harmondsworth: Penguin.

Moss, L. (1979) Overview. In L. Moss and H. Goldstein (eds) *The Recall Method in Social Surveys* (pp. 159–169). University of London, Institute of Education, London.

Moura, Castro (1987) Is vocational education really that bad? *International Labour Review* 126 (5), 603–610.

Murgatroyd, L. (1982) Gender and occupational stratification. *Sociological Review* 30 (4), 572–602.

National Economic Development Council (NEDC) (1992) *UK Tourism: Competing for Growth*. London: National Economic Development Council.

NLG (1995) Towards a core curriculum for tourism: A discussion paper. Guideline Number 1 (written by Chris Holloway).

Neisser, U. (1967) *Cognitive Psychology*. New York: Appleton-Century-Crofts.

Neisser, U. (1978) Memory: What are the important questions? In M.M. Gruneberg, P.E. Morris. and R.N. Sykes (eds) *Practical Aspects of Memory*. London: Academic Press.

Nickenson, R.S. (ed.) *Attention and Performance* (VIII, pp. 651–699). Hillside NJ: Erlbaum.

Norman, D.A. and Bobrow, D.G. (1979) Descriptions: An intermediate stage in memory retrieval. *Cognitive Psychology* 11, 107–123.

Pavesic, D.V. (1993a) Hospitality education 2005: Curricular and programmatic trends. *Hospitality Research Journal* 17 (1), 285–294.

Pavesic, D.V. (1993b) Programmatic issues in undergraduate hospitality education. *Hospitality and Tourism Educator*, 38–51.

Peters, H.E. (1989) Retrospective versus panel data in analysing life cycle events. *Journal of Human Resources* 23 (40), 201–213.

Pike, R. (1994) It pays to juggle with your work. *The Daily Telegraph*, 20 September, p. 15.

Pizam, A. (1982) Tourism manpower: The state of the art. *Journal of Travel Research* 21, 5–9.

Prais, S.J., Jarvis, J. and Wagner, K. (1989) Productivity and vocational skills in services in Britain and Germany: Hotels. *National Institute Economic Review*, November, 52–74.

Price, J. and Mueller, C. (1981) *Professional Turnover: The Case of Nurses*. New York: SP Medical Books.

Psacharopoulos, G. (1991a) From manpower planning to labour market analysis. *International Labour Review* 130 (4), 459–469.

Psacharopoulos, G. (1991b) Vocational education theory, VOCED 101: Including hints for vocational planners. *International Journal of Educational Development* 11, 193–199.

Pukli, P. (1994) Szerkezeti változások a fôbb gazdasági ágazatokban, 1989–1993. *Statisztikai Szemle* 72 (10), 709–721.

Reeb, M. (1959) How people see jobs: A multi dimensional analysis. *Occupational Psychology* 33 (1), 1–17.

Reed, K. (1997) Orientations to work: The cultural conditioning of motivation. *Australian and New Zealand Journal of Sociology* 33 (3), 364–386.

Reiser, B.J., Black, J.B. and Abelson, R.P. (1985) Knowledge structures in the organization and retrieval of autobiographical memories. *Cognitive Psychology* 17 (1), 89–137.

Reiser, B.J., Black, J.B. and Kalamarides, P. (1986) Strategic memory search processes. In D.C. Rubin (ed.) *Autobiographical Memory* (pp. 100–121). Cambridge: Cambridge University Press.

Riley, M. (1986a) A social psychological framework for customer service training. *Tourism Management* 7, 103–112.

Riley, M. (1986b) Some social and historical perspective on unionization in the UK hotel industry. *International Journal of Hospitality Management* 14 (3), 99–104.

Riley, M. (1990) The labour retention strategies of UK hotel managers. *The Service Industries Journal* 10 (3), 614–618.

Riley, M. (1990) The role of age distributions in career path analysis. *International Journal of Tourism Management* 11 (3), 38–44.

Riley, M. (1991a) An analysis of hotel labour markets. In C. Cooper (ed.) *Progress in Tourism, Recreation and Hospitality Management* (3, Ch. 14, pp. 232–246). London: Belhaven Press.

Riley, M. (1991b) *Human Resource Management: A Guide to Personnel Practice in the Hotel and Catering Industry* (Ch. 20) Oxford: Butterworth-Heinemann.

Riley, M. (1993a) Age distributions as a tracer study. *International Journal of Manpower* 14 (1), 34–39.

Riley, M. (1993b) Industrial relations in the hotel industry. In C. Cooper (ed.) *Progress in Tourism, Recreation and Hospitality Management* (5, Ch. 14, pp. 242–247). London: Belhaven Press.

Riley, M. (1993c) Labour markets and vocational education In T. Baum (ed.) *Human Resource Issues in Tourism* (Ch. 4, pp. 47–59). Oxford: Butterworth-Heinemann.

Riley, M. (1995a) Analysis of managerial experience: Integrating career analysis with labour market dynamics. *British Journal of Management* 6, 95–203.

Riley, M. (1995b) Interpersonal communication: The contribution of dyadic analysis to the understanding of tourism behaviour. *Progress in Tourism and Hospitality Research* 1 (2), 115–124.

Riley, M. (1996) *Human Resource Management in the Hospitality and Tourism Industry* (2nd edn). Oxford: Butterworth-Heinemann.

Riley, M. (1997) Motivational strategies in Eastern Europe: The special case of service workers. In M. Foley, J. Lennon and G. Maxwell (eds) *Hospitality, Tourism and Leisure Management: Issues in Strategy and Culture.* London: Cassell.

Riley, M. (1999) Re-defining the debate on hospitality productivity. *Tourism and Hospitality Research* 1 (2), 182–186.

Riley, M. (2000) *Managing People* (2nd edn, Ch. 16). Oxford: Butterworth-Heinemann.

Riley, M., Gore, J. and Kelliher, C. (2000) Economic determinism and human resource management practice in the hospitality and tourism industry. *Tourism and Hospitality Research* 2 (2), 118–128.

Riley, M. and Ladkin, A. (1994) Career theory and tourism: The development of a basic analytical framework. *Progress in Tourism, Recreation and Hospitality Management* 6, 225–237.

Riley, M. and Lockwood, A. (1997) Strategies and measurement for workforce flexibility: An application of functional flexibility in a service setting. *International Journal of Operations and Productivity Management* 17 (4), 413–419.

Riley, M., Lockwood, A., Powell-Perry, J. and Baker M. (1998) Job satisfaction, organisation commitment and occupational culture: A case from the UK pub industry. *Progress in Tourism and Hospitality Research* 4, 159–168.

Robinson, J.A. (1976) Sampling and autobiographical memory. *Cognitive Psychology* 8, 578–595.

Robinson, J.A. (1986) Autobiographical memory: A historical prologue. In D.C. Rubin (ed.) *Autobiographical Memory* (pp. 19–24). Cambridge: Cambridge University Press.

Robinson, J.A. (1992) Autobiographical memory. In M. Gruneberg and P. Morris. (eds) *Aspects of Memory. The Practical Aspects* (2nd edn, 1, pp. 223–251). London: Routledge.

Robinson, J.A. and Swanson, K.L. (1990) Autobiographical memory: The next phase. *Applied Cognitive Psychology* 4 (4), 321–335

Rogers, T. B., Kuiper, N.A. and Kirker, W.S. (1977) Self-reference and the encoding of personal information. *Journal of Personality and Social Psychology* 25 (9), 677–688.

Roseman, I. (1984) Cognitive determinants of emotion. In P. Shaner (ed.) *Review of Personality and Social Psychology* (5, pp. 11–36). Beverly Hills: Sage.

Rosen, S. (1972) Learning and experience in the Labor Market. *Journal of Human Resources* 7 (4), 326–342.

Rousseau, D.M. (1995) *Psychological Contracts in Organizations.* London: Sage.

Rubin, D.C. (1982) On the retention function for autobiographical memory. *Journal of Verbal Learning and Verbal Behavior* 21, 21–38.

Rubin, D.C., Witzler, S.E. and Nebes, R.D. (1986) Autobiographical memory across the lifespan. In D.C. Rubin (ed.) *Autobiographical Memory* (pp. 202–221). Cambridge: Cambridge University Press.

Salaman, G. (1974) *Community and Occupation*. Cambridge: Cambridge University Press.

Salancik, G. R. and Pfeffer, J. (1978) A social information processing approach to job attitudes and task design. *Administrative Science Quarterly* 23, 224–253.

Salleh, H. (1995) A study of the career paths of chefs in Malaysia. Unpublished PhD thesis. University of Surrey, Guildford.

Salleh, H. and Riley, M. (1994) Measuring culinary learning processes: Education and experience contrasted. *International Journal of Contemporary Hospitality Management* 6 (6), iii–v.

Samenfink, W.H. (1992). A rebuttal: Careerism and general education revisited in the hospitality curriculum. *Hospitality and Tourism Educator* 4 (40), 50–52.

Saunders, K.C. (1981) *Social Stigma of Occupations*. Farnborough: Gower.

Schein, E.H. (1975) How career anchors hold executives to their career paths. *Personnel* 52 (3) 11–24.

Schein, E.H. (1978) *Career Dynamics: Matching Individual and Organisational Needs*. London: Addison-Wesley.

Schroeder, L. (1976) Interrelatedness of occupational and geographical labour mobility. *Industrial and Labour Relations Review* 29, 411–435.

Shamir, B. (1980) Between service and servility, role conflict in subordinate service roles. *Human Relations* 33, 741–756.

Shamir, B. (1981) The workplace as a community: The case of British hotels. *Industrial Relations Journal* 12 (6), 45–56.

Shapira, Z. (1981) Making trade-offs between job attributes. *Organizational Behaviour and Human Performance* 28 (3), 331–355.

Shaw, G. and Williams, A.M. (1994) *Critical Issues in Tourism: A Geographical Perspective*. Oxford: Blackwell.

Simms, J., Hales, C. and Riley, M. (1988) Examination of the concept of internal labour markets in UK hotels. *International Journal of Tourism Management* 9 (3), 63–78.

Sindiga, I. (1994) Employment and training in tourism in Kenya. *The Journal of Tourism Studies* 5 (2), 45–52.

Singer, J.A. (1990) Affective responses to autobiographical memories and their relationship to long term goals. *Journal of Personality* 53 (3), 535–563.

Skowronski, J.J., Thompson, C.P., Betz, A.L. and Shannon, L. (1991) Social memory in everday life: Recall of self-events and other events. *Journal of Personality and Social Psychology* 60 (6), 831–843.

Slichter, S. (1950) Notes on the structure of wages. *Review of Economics and Statistics* 32, 80–91.

Smith, A. (1976) *The Wealth of Nations*. Harmondsworth: Penguin (original work published 1776).

Smith, A.R. (1976a) The philosophy of manpower planning. In D. Bartholomew (ed.) *Manpower Planning* (Ch. 2). Harmondsworth: Penguin.

Smith, A.R. (1976b) What is manpower planning? In D. Bartholomew (ed.) *Manpower Planning* (Ch. 4). Harmondsworth: Penguin.

Smith S.L.J. (1988) Defining tourism – A supply-side view. *Annals of Tourism Research* 15 (2), 179–190.

Stinchcombe, A.L. (1963) Some empirical consequences of the Davis-Moore theory of stratification. *American Sociological Review* 38, 805–808.
Storper, M. and Scott, A. J. (1990) Work organisation and local labour markets in an era of flexible production. *International Labour Review* 129 (5), 573–592.
Stumpf, S.A., Colarelli, S.M. and Hartman, K. (1983) Development of the career exploration survey (CES). *Journal of Vocational Behavior* 22, 191–226.
Szivas E. (1999) The influence of human resources on tourism marketing. In F. Vellas and L. Becherel (eds) *The International Marketing of Travel and Tourism: A Strategic Approach.* London: Macmillan.
Szivas, E. and Riley, M. (1999) Tourism employment in conditions of economic transition: The case of Hungary. *Annals of Tourism Research* 26 (4), 747–771
Thompson, C.P. (1982) Memory for unique personal events: The roommate study. *Memory and Cognition* 10 (4), 324–332.
Thompson, C.P. (1985) Memory for unique personal events: Some implication of the self-schema. *Human Learning* 4 (4), 267–280.
Thompson, C.P., Skowronski, J.J. and Lee, D.J. (1988) Reconstructing the date of a personal event. In M.M. Gruneberg, P.E. Morris. and R.N. Sykes (eds) *Practical Aspects of Memory: Current Research and Issues* (1, pp. 241–246). Chichester: John Wiley and Sons.
The Tourism Society (1981) *Employment in the Tourism Industry for School Leavers.* London: The Tourism Society.
Tribe, J. (2000) Balancing the vocational: The theory and practice of liberal education in tourism. *Tourism and Hospitality Research* 2 (1), 9–25.
Truss, C., Gratton, L., Hope-Hailey,V., McGovern P. and Stiles P. (1997) Soft and hard models of human resource management: A reappraisal. *Journal of Management Studies* 34 (1), 53–73.
Tulving, E. (1972) Episodic and semantic memory. In E. Tulving and W. Donaldson (eds) *Organisation of Memory.* New York: Academic Press.
Tuma, N.B. (1976) Rewards, resources and the rate of mobility: A non-stationary multivariate stochastic model. *American Sociological Review* 41(2), 338–360.
Urry, J. (1990) *The Tourist Gaze.* London: Sage Publications.
Van Maanen, J. (1977) *Organisational Careers: Some New Perspectives.* London: John Wiley and Sons.
Watson, K. (1994) Technical and vocational education in developing countries: Western paradigms and comparative methodology. *Comparative Education* 30 (2), 85–97.
Weiner, B. (1982) The emotional consequences of causal attributions. In M.S. Clark and S.T. Fiske (eds) *Affect and Cognition* (pp. 185–209). Hillside, NJ: Lawrence Erlbaum.
Weiner, B. (1985) An attributional theory of achievement motivation and emotion. *Psychological Review* 92, 548–573.
Weiner, B., Russel, D. and Lerman, D. (1979) The cognition-emotion process in achievement – related contacts. *Journal of Personality and Social Psychology* 40, 650–663.
Wharton A.S. (1993) The affective consequences of service work: Managing emotions on the job. *Work and Occupations* 20 (2), 205–232.
Whitten, W.B. and Leonard, J.M. (1981) Directed search through autobiographical memory over six years. *Cognitive Psychology* 18, 225–52.

Williams, M.L. and Leppel, K. (1994) Modelling occupational choice in blue-collar labor markets. *Economics of Education Review* 13 (3), 243–250.

Willis, P. (1979) Shop floor cultures, masculinity and wage norms. In J.K. Clarke (ed.) *Working Class Culture.* London: Hutchinson.

Wilson, K.L. and Portes, A. (1980) Immigrant enclaves: An analysis of the labour market experiences of Cubans in Miami. *American Journal of Sociology* 86 (2), 295–319.

Wood, R.C. (1992) *Working in Hotels and Catering.* London: Routledge.

World Tourism Organisation (1983) *Tourism Employment: Enhancing the Status of Tourism Professions.* Madrid: World Tourism Organisation.

Wyer, R.S., Shoben, E.J., Fuhrman, R.W. and Bodenhausen, G.V. (1985) Event theory: The temporal organization of social action sequences. *Journal of Personality and Social Psychology* 49, 857–877.

Yarrow, M.R., Campbell, J.D. and Burton, R.V. (1970) Recollections of childhood: A study of the retrospective method. *Monographs of the Society for Research in Child Development* 35 (5).

Zola-Morgan, S., Cohen, N.J. and Squire, L.R. (1983) Recall of remote episodic memory in amnesia. *Neuropsychologia* 21, 487–500.

Index

Urry 23
Van Maanen 112
Virtual market wage 44
Vocational education and
    development
– and experience 171-173
– relevance of 184

Wall 24, 26
Watson 184
Way of life 38
Weiner 86

Wharton 66
Whitten 79
Williams 12, 24, 26, 183
Willis 65
Wilson 36
Wood 25
World Tourism Organisation 12, 23
Wyer 87

Yarrow 88

Zola-Morgan 81